The Last Laugh

"Will a day come when the race will detect the funniness of these juvenilities and laugh at them—and by laughing at them destroy them? For your race, in its poverty, has unquestionably one really effective weapon—laughter. Power, Money, Persuasion, Supplication, Persecution—these can lift at a colossal humbug,—push it a little—crowd it a little—weaken it a little, century by century: but only Laughter can blow it to rags and atoms at a blast.

—Mark Twain, *The Mysterious Stranger*

The Last Laugh

Form and Affirmation in the Contemporary American Comic Novel

Ronald Wallace

University of Missouri Press
Columbia & London, 1979

University of Missouri Press, Columbia, Missouri 65211
Library of Congress Catalog Card Number 78–21376
Printed and bound in the United States of America

Library of Congress Cataloging in Publication Data

Wallace, Ronald, 1945–.
The last laugh.

Bibliography: p. 149.
Includes index.
1. American fiction—20th century—History and criticism. 2. Comic, The. I. Title.
PS379.W293 813'.03 78–21376
ISBN 0–8262–0274–8

Chapter I is a revised version of an article that originally appeared in *Texas Studies in Literature and Language*. (Wallace, Ronald. "Never Mind that the Nag's a Pile of Bones: The Modern Comic Novel and the Comic Tradition." *Texas Studies in Literature and Language* 19, no. 1 [Spring 1977]:1–23.) Material used by permission of the University of Texas Press.

For my family

Acknowledgments

I would like to thank Professors William Gibson, Walter Rideout, and Merton Sealts for their kind support and encouragement. I also wish gratefully to acknowledge the American Council of Learned Societies for a fellowship, and the Graduate School Research Committee of the University of Wisconsin for a grant that supported the writing of this book. Portions of the book originally appeared in *Essays in Literature*, *Studies in the Novel*, and *Texas Studies in Literature and Language*. I wish to thank the editors of those journals for permission to reprint material that appears here in altered and expanded form.

Contents

I.

Never Mind that the Nag's a Pile of Bones

The Contemporary American Comic Novel and the Comic Tradition

1.

"Bombs and bomb throwers we've got," lamented Melvin Maddocks in a 1970 *Time* article. "But where are the pies? Where are those pie throwers?"[1] Maddocks argues that American society in particular, and the modern world in general, has forgotten how to laugh. Indeed, if one were to catalogue the defining characteristics of twentieth-century life, the comic spirit would probably be far down the list. We tend to define ourselves in terms of war, violence, sickness, despair, loss, guilt, and social and political fragmentation, rather than laughter. Given the ugliness of the Vietnam War, racial prejudice, urban unrest, governmental duplicity, and ecological and economic crises, anxiety and outrage may seem the only appropriate responses, and the only conceivable laughter, a hollow, cynical laughter.

Nevertheless, comedy has become the characteristic form of the contemporary American novel, a comedy that incorporates the violence and chaos of modern life. Wylie Sypher suggests that the very extremity of our experience provides the necessary foundation for a new appreciation of the comic:

> We have, in short, been forced to admit that the absurd is more than ever inherent in human existence: that is, the irrational, the inexplicable, the surprising, the nonsensical—in other words, the comic. . . . The modern hero lives amid irreconcilables which . . . can be encompassed only by religious faith—or comedy. . . . Is it any wonder that along with our wars, our machines, and our neuroses we should find new meanings in comedy, or that comedy should represent our plight better than tragedy?[2]

Faced with a world in which the grotesque, the trivial, and the preposterous seem to rule, novelists like John Barth, John Hawkes, Vladimir Nabokov, Ken Kesey, Robert Coover, and others affirm laughter as a weapon against defeat and despair. In the course of a typical contemporary novel, the hero and his adversaries engage in a series of metaphoric pie-throwing contests that ultimately restore a sense of comic perspective, if not always to the hero or his society, then to the reader. Occasionally, the restoration even takes the form of a crash course in laughter. In Kesey's *One Flew Over the Cuckoo's Nest*, for example, the hero, McMurphy, restores balance and hope to the inmates of the mental hospital by teaching them how to laugh. James Purdy's *Cabot Wright Begins* provides a virtual recipe for laughter: "First Ha then Ho, than Ha Ha HAR, HAAAAAA!"[3] If the recent comic novel lacks the didacticism typical of some earlier comedy, it retains a firm belief in the importance of a comic perspective on the self and society.

Until recently, however, literary critics have not devoted much serious attention to the comic element of the modern novel. As Louis Rubin observes, "The industry and prodigality of modern-day American literary scholarship being what they are, it may seem strange that so little writing has been done about so vast a subject."[4] There are perhaps several reasons for the critical neglect. Writing on E. M. Forster, Lionel Trilling observes, "Nowadays even the literate reader is likely to be unschooled in the comic tradition and unaware of the comic seriousness."[5] Having accepted the idea that comedy somehow deals with less serious subject matter than tragedy and is therefore an inferior art form, an idea derived or distorted from Aristotle, many modern critics have focused on other elements of the novel, relegating comedy to the realm of escape or momentary relief from the pressures of "reality." A second possible reason for the neglect is that comedy is difficult to write about. To analyze humor, some critics maintain, is to destroy it. A joke explained is no longer a joke. Thus there is something awkward, even embarrassing, about describing the comic: the writer himself is always precariously perched on the edge of self-parody; he risks becoming the kind of humorless pedant that Pope and Fielding were so fond of satirizing.

Recently, however, critics have turned their attention to comedy, in part because the contemporary novel is inescapably comic and in part because recent novelists themselves have directed attention to the comic form. Most critics now accept the term *black humor* as descriptive of the contemporary novel, and most critics acknowledge the comic method characteristic of the best recent novelists. But many critics also embrace two erroneous assumptions about black humor: first, that it is "new," and a purely American phenomenon; second, that the emphasis should be on *black* rather than *humor*.

The term *black humor* was not, of course, invented by Conrad Knickerbocker in 1964, as some critics seem to assume;[6] it originated with André Breton, who compiled an *Anthologie de l'humour noir* in 1939. Defining black humor as a means by which an individual could defend his inner self against the physical, psychological, and social constraints of the human condition, Breton included in his anthology such writers as Swift, Poe, Baudelaire, Lewis Carroll, and Kafka. Far from being a new creation, black humor represents an outgrowth of an observable comic tradition, the recognition of which is necessary for valid interpretation.

John Barth wryly points up the importance of this comic tradition in his own writing and in that of other recent novelists. When asked whether the "emerging of a new kind of comic novel" held any interest for him, Barth replied, "It holds interest for me because I thought I had invented it, and now it turns out that somebody else got there first. Rabelais. Machado. It depresses the Dickens out of me." When asked to name some younger writers whose work has been neglected, Barth listed "Boccaccio, Cervantes, Rabelais . . . Laurence Sterne, also Machado de Assis. . . . If you don't know them [the novels of Machado] already and you're interested in this new genre that I invented, you should surely read Machado, because he invented it too."[7] Barth is, of course, ridiculing the notion that the recent comic novel was invented by anybody; it is a development in a long tradition of comic writing.

If many critics fail to recognize the tradition in which the modern comic novel participates, they also fail to emphasize the comedy implied by the term *black humor*, preferring to emphasize the blackness. Max Schulz, for example, in the one full-length study of black humor, rather feebly justifies his failure to examine the comedy. "I have shied away from the 'humor' in Black Humor. Most efforts to come to terms with the comic over the past two thousand years have drifted into the shallows of laughter and foundered on the submerged rocks of psychology's attempts to explain why we chuckle. Hence my timidity. Secondly, to give equal value to humor in any consideration of this literature is possibly to let oneself be trapped by a term that came into being somewhat capriciously and may not accurately describe that literature."[8] Schulz's arguments are the usual ones: it is difficult to write about comedy, and the contemporary novel is not really comic after all. Bruce Janoff, in an attempt to define black humor, takes Schulz's assumptions even further. "Discounting the comic element for a moment, then, it would follow that black humor can be roughly equated with tragedy." The black humor novelist has, Janoff concludes, "an overwhelmingly tragic view of the world."[9]

Most recent novelists, however, describe their work in terms that unmistakably emphasize the importance of comedy and the comic tradition. Robert Coover observes, "I tend to think of tragedy as a kind of adolescent response to the universe—the higher truth is a comic response."[10] John Hawkes insists, "reviewers in general have concentrated on the grotesque and nightmarish qualities of my work, have made me out to be a somber writer dealing only with pain, perversion, and despair. Comedy puts all this into a very different perspective. . . . Comic distortion tells us that anything is possible and hence expands the limits of our imaginations. Comic vision always suggests futurity, I think, always suggests a certain hope in the limitless energies of life itself."[11] Taking its place in a recognizable comic tradition, the contemporary American comic novel reflects the form, themes, and characteristic devices of earlier comedy.

E. D. Hirsch, in his *Validity in Interpretation*, insists that "an interpreter's preliminary generic conception of a text is constitutive of everything that he subsequently understands, and . . . this remains the case unless and until that generic conception is altered."[12] Generically confusing black humor with tragedy or irony, critics have inadequately analyzed its comic tone and spirit.[13] For this reason I have chosen to replace the term *black humor* with the more accurate and less misleading description, "contemporary American comic novel," and this study will attempt to describe the generic, recurring, and conventional aspects of comedy that inform the novels. An archetypal analysis of the "intrinsic genre" of the recent comic novel reveals its position in the comic tradition, and suggests its participation in the comic affirmation typical of the form.

2.

According to Aristotle, tragedy is structured primarily on plot, and comedy on character. Although a rich variety of characters is evident in the comic tradition, most comic protagonists resemble one of two conventional archetypes, the *eiron* or the *alazon* of Old Comedy. According to Northrop Frye, the *eiron* is the witty self-deprecator, predestined to be an artist, who ridicules the more narrow *alazons* of his comic society. The *alazon* is the boastful antagonist, the impostor or fool who pretends to be more than he really is. The conflict of *eiron* and *alazon*, of wit and fool, of self-knowledge and self-deception, usually structures the comic plot.[14] Of course, the antitheses are not always so clearly drawn, especially in recent fiction. At its most complex, the contemporary American comic novel combines the two types. The comic conflict is then an inner one, between warring aspects of the hero's psyche. The personalities of Elkin's Feldman, Baker's Shillitoe, Friedman's Stern, Kesey's McMurphy, Nabokov's Humbert Humbert, Barth's Todd Andrews, Hawkes's Skipper, Donleavy's Sebastian Dangerfield, and Coover's J. Henry Waugh subtly combine elements of self-deprecation and egotism, artistry and exposure. This fusion of conventional types is one distinguishing feature of the recent comic novel.

In the past, the comic hero has typically been a fool or buffoon, a self-deceived character. Jane Austen's Emma, for example, is obviously misguided, selfish, egotistical, and naive, and the comedy derives from the conflict between the deluded heroine and her more intelligent foil, Knightley, the witty, self-deprecating *eiron* and representative of Highbury society. Eventually, of course, Knightley's comic wit punctures Emma's delusions, and the heroine joyously embraces the social norms of reason and balance. More extreme characters in the *alazon* tradition are Swift's mad narrators in *The Tale of a Tub* and *A Modest Proposal*, and Henry James's narrator in *The Sacred Fount*. Obsessed by their curious delusions, these characters expose themselves in ways they can't comprehend, failing finally to be converted or reformed.

Like Austen's, Swift's, and James's protagonists, the contemporary American comic hero seems at first to derive primarily from the *alazon* archetype. Nabokov's Humbert Humbert, for example, boasts of his devoted love for his stepdaughter throughout *Lolita*, while unconsciously exposing the falsity of his claims; John Hawkes's Skipper insists on his innocence in a world full of violence and ugliness without ever realizing that his very innocence contributes to the pain he abhors; Barth's Todd Andrews claims to run his life according to reason, never perceiving that his reliance on reason is itself unreasonable and that his decision to commit suicide is less rational than emotional. The discrepancy between the characters' interpretations of their situation and the reader's perception of it is comic.

The comic potential of unconscious self-exposure is increased when the hero himself is cast as the narrator in his own fiction. The narrative strategy of having the protagonist tell his own story has become an increasingly popular one in the contemporary novel, and it is comic in several ways. For one thing, the reader can assume from the outset that everything is going to turn out all right in the end. *Great Expectations* provides a good example from earlier fiction. In that novel, Pip relates the story of his youth from the perspective of age. As a wiser man, he is able to look back on his previous foolishness with a comic detachment that combines ridicule and sympathy. Also, since Pip has obviously lived to tell his story, the reader's response to the frightening and violent events of Pip's earlier life are tempered. The question necessarily becomes not what will happen to Pip in the end, but rather how he gets to that end, what happens on the way, and why. Barth and Hawkes use the same narrative strategy in *The Floating Opera* and *Second Skin*. Although Todd's novel is about his attempted suicide, the reader knows from the outset of *The Floating Opera* that Todd will live. While Skipper's novel focuses on a progression of violence and terror, Skipper narrates *Second Skin* from the perspective of a pastoral Pacific island, indicating his eventual escape from the world of death that surrounds him. Thus, the first-person novel usually provides the comic assurance that the character will survive, will indeed prevail to the point that he can craft a work of art. The fact that the narrator casts himself in the role of a naive or deluded protagonist suggests that he, like Pip and Emma, has gained a measure of comic perspective on his earlier experience.

But the narrative strategy of making the hero the author of his own novel has a more complex comic potential. Since the narrator is intimately involved in his own story, he does not possess the critical detachment of an omniscient author like

Jane Austen or George Meredith. Therefore, it is possible that the narrator's later observations are either just as deluded as his earlier actions or are conscious lies. The comic convention of the unreliable narrator has been a favorite with recent novelists, who have cast liars, fools, knaves, madmen, and computers in the role of narrator, subverting the reader's expectations of authorial integrity. Of course, many of the great comic characters in earlier literature have been liars. Falstaff and Huck Finn are obvious examples, the comedy in their cases deriving from the discrepancy between the reader's perception of the lie and the victim's naive acceptance of the lie as truth. Huck Finn's accounts of his suffering are comic not only because of their obvious exaggeration, but also because everyone else in the novel believes them. At one point in *Huckleberry Finn*, for example, Huck explains:

> I told them how pap and me and all the family was living on a little farm down at the bottom of Arkansaw, and my sister Mary Ann run off and got married and never was heard of no more, and Bill went off to hunt them, and he warn't heard of no more, and Tom and Mort died, and then there warn't nobody but just me and pap left, and he was just trimmed down to nothing, on account of his troubles; so when he died I took what there was left, because the farm didn't belong to us, and started up the river, deck passage, and fell overboard; and that was how I come to be here.[15]

J. P. Donleavy employs the same comic device in his more recent picaresque novel, *The Ginger Man.* After getting drunk and starting a brawl in a bar, the hero, Sebastian Dangerfield, describes the episode:

> Most ungentlemanly incident I think I've ever experienced. . . . I went into this public house for a quiet drink. Stone cold sober. Man seizes me by the arm and twists it—says get out—you're drunk. I said, I beg your pardon but I'm stone. Naturally I left under the maltreatment that was in it. Now I'm not an evil person, nor do I ever encourage any type of trouble. However I returned to this bar later, ordered another drink and they attacked me brutally. Disgraceful behavior. All on me like a pack of wolves. Trying to put me down and jump on me. It was only by employing the most elusive tactics that I succeeded in escaping

> with my very life. I have no doubts but that they are searching the city to visit me with more abuse.[16]

The discrepancy between Dangerfield's exaggerated description of his victimization and the reality of the situation is comic, and the fact that people so readily believe his eloquent lies intensifies the comedy.

In Huck's and Sebastian's cases the lies are fairly easy to detect; indeed, detection is necessary for an appreciation of the comedy. In most recent novels with duplicitous narrators, however, the lies are not so obvious. In fact, narrators like Barth's Todd Andrews and Nabokov's Humbert Humbert do all they can to prevent the reader from perceiving their lies. Todd Andrews, for example, in an effort to gain reader sympathy, consciously misleads the reader in much the same way that Huck and Dangerfield mislead the characters in their novels. Only by perceiving the subtle contradictions between Todd's words and his actions, between his analysis of events and their actual significance, can the reader interpret Todd correctly. For example, when Todd insists that he is an inept writer who knows nothing about literary devices and then *uses* those very devices repeatedly, the reader must be skeptical of his other claims. The reader who accepts Todd's interpretations at face value becomes the butt of the joke.

Sometimes the narrator himself is fooled by his own duplicity. For example, Humbert Humbert, a lecher, murderer, blackmailer, pervert, thief, liar, and madman by his own assessment, often sincerely believes his own lies. He believes, for example, his claim that he wants only happiness for Lolita, but it is evident from his actions that he wants only satisfaction for himself. Although Humbert cannot admit it, his invention of the concept of *nymphet* is primarily a justification for his own lust. In this respect, Humbert rather closely resembles Swift's mad narrator in *A Modest Proposal* and James's mad narrator in *The Sacred Fount*. Like his predecessors, Humbert takes a single case and posits from it a general law. In *A Modest Proposal*, babies are edible; in *The Sacred Fount*, people are vampires; in *Lolita*, certain small girls are nymphets. If we admit the absurd postulates, then we must accept the conclusions. But the reader is expected to bring to bear on the stories a set of assumptions and values that reject the postulates. It is wrong to eat babies; people are not vampires; there are no such things as nymphets.

3.

If, in his role as comic *alazon*, the contemporary American comic hero is often a boaster, liar, and self-deceived impostor who exposes himself in ways he doesn't suspect, he is also, in his role as *eiron*, an able and witty critic of his society, reflecting the ambivalence Dale Underwood observes is typical of the greatest comic heroes:

> It is an essential of the comic hero . . . that he have this ambivalence. His attitudes and actions serve, on the one hand, to criticize his society; but they serve on the other to criticize himself. If they do only the former, the character is not comic; if they do only the latter, he is no hero. As an aspect of his ambivalence of character his wit, if he has any, will also be ambivalent. It may sometimes operate to minify his society—and then we laugh with him, or it may sometimes serve to minify him—and then we laugh at him. But it may simultaneously do both, and then the comic complexity of both character and language is at its peak.[17]

The contemporary comic hero criticizes his society in two basic ways: by ridiculing a single humor figure who personifies the humorous society and by satirically exposing the mechanistic and arbitrary assumptions on which the society is based.

When Ihab Hassan claims that "there are no pure villains" in literature, he rejects one obvious and important device that comic writers have traditionally used to combat evil.[18] Evil exerts a powerful force in most comedy, and a writer has a number of methods for dealing with it. He can treat it as impotent, as a temporary aberration that ultimately gives way to happy results. Such treatment generates typical romantic comedies, like those of Shakespeare. Alternately, a writer can create a character who surmounts evil and suffering by rising above it through sheer moral excellence, as is typical of the comedies of Henry James. In the contemporary comic novel, evil is rarely either converted or overcome; instead it is controlled, if rather tenuously and precariously, through satiric laughter. Evil in the contemporary American comic novel is often felt as a dark power loose in the universe, a vague, undefinable, intractable force that pervades modern life and takes shape in society and its institutions. It is the force that oils Kesey's "Combine" and drives Joseph Heller's military machine. It is the force that erupts with such unexpected violence in the novels of John Hawkes.[19] By portraying this abstract evil as a concrete comic villain, the comic novelist undercuts its potentially destructive power.

The caricature of pure evil appears in nearly every modern comic novel, and it is the hero's job to ridicule or evade it. Personifying what is worst in the humorous society, the comic villain is often typed by a comic name. From Dickens's Magwitch, through Joyce's Nasty Roche and Blazes Boylan, Forster's Major Callendar, Kesey's Big Nurse, Heller's General Scheisskopf, Hawkes's Tremlow, Barth's John Coode, Nabokov's Clare Quilty, Vonnegut's Norman Mushari, Friedman's kike man, and Coover's Horace Zifferblatt, the humor villain tries to force the comic plot into compliance with his destructive obsession. In most cases the hero manages to escape the full consequences of evil by controlling it through a comic perspective. As J. Henry Waugh remarks, "how could anyone take seriously, after all, a man named Horace Zifferblatt?"[20] Even when the hero seems ultimately "defeated" by the humor villain, as in the case of Leopold Bloom, Humbert Humbert, Stern, and McMurphy, the hero's comic exposure of the villain is itself a "triumph," enabling the *reader* to laugh at a society ruled by inhuman and irrational laws.

Henri Bergson's definition of the comic as "the mechanical encrusted on the living" thus describes the society that confronts the recent comic hero.[21] In a world where most people behave rigidly and mechanically, the protagonist distinguishes himself by his fluidity and eccentricity. In earlier comedy, though the protagonist might be deluded, the society was often sane and reasonable. In the contemporary comic novel the situation is characteristically reversed. Now the hero, deluded though he may be, is more sane than his society. This is not new, of course. The same situation obtains in *Don Quixote*, where the Don's "madness" is obviously preferable to the world's "sanity," in James's *The Spoils of Poynton*, where Fleda Vetch's misinterpretations are more beautiful and life-affirming than the "reality" of her London society, and in Dickens's *Great Expectations*, where Pip's youthful egotism is never as dehumanizing as the rigidity of his world.

The world of the contemporary comic novel, like Dickens's England, transforms people into things and things into people.

In *One Flew Over the Cuckoo's Nest*, Nurse Ratched is as mechanical as her name implies, and in *The Universal Baseball Association*, Horace Zifferblatt reflects the clockwork of his German name. In Thomas Pynchon's *V*, human beings have become very much like the SHOCKS (Synthetic Human Object, Casualty Kinematics) with which Benny Profane works. Benny feels "a certain kinship with SHOCK, which was the first inanimate schlemihl he'd ever encountered."[22] And in Heller's *Catch-22*, Lieutenant Scheisskopf wants "to have a friend of his in the sheet metal shop sink pegs of nickel alloy into each man's thighbones and link them to the wrists by strands of copper wire with exactly three inches of play" to improve his unit's marching efficiency.[23]

While the stock figures surrounding the protagonist grow increasingly inert and mechanical, inanimate objects take on mysterious life. In *Lolita*, motel rooms seem to conspire against Humbert, and the car that kills Charlotte Haze has "doors open like wings," while an old man involved in the accident is as inert as a wax doll. In *Second Skin*, Miranda's black brassiere takes on a malicious life of its own, dangling like an albatross from a hook on Red's boat. In *The Crying of Lot 49*, Oedipa Maas's aerosol can of hair spray goes berserk, crashing about the room of its own accord; in *Giles Goat-Boy*, Miss Hector loses her virginity to WESCAC, a machine.

The satire of this inversion of the human and the inanimate often extends to the commercialism that seems to be a cause or result of the reversal. In *Lolita*, for example, Humbert satirizes his nymphet as the perfect consumer:

> She believed, with a kind of celestial trust, any advertisement or advice that appeared in *Movie Love* or *Screen Land*. . . . If a roadside sign said: VISIT OUR GIFT SHOP—we *had* to visit it, *had* to buy its Indian curios, dolls, copper jewelry, cactus candy. The words "novelties and souvenirs" simply entranced her by their trochaic lilt. If some café sign proclaimed Icecold Drinks, she was automatically stirred, although all drinks everywhere were ice-cold. She it was to whom ads were dedicated: the ideal consumer, the subject and object of every foul poster.[24]

Similarly, in *Cabot Wright Begins*, Purdy satirically attacks American consumerism. America "has ended in a shambles of scrofulous obscenity and barking half-breeds in which nothing worth selling or connecting is hawked, barked, and exposed in its inadequate meretricious shine to a nation of uninterested buyers. . . . America's single role at present is to militate confusion, dirt, hollowness, race transvestism, so that she can pass as quickly as possible into the cosmic scrap-hole of non-existence."[25] In Terry Southern's *The Magic Christian*, the "grand guy Guy Grand" viciously exposes America's lust for money and things. At one point in the novel, Grand fills an enormous cauldron with boiling excrement and money, and watches the people scramble through the muck, dehumanizing themselves in the pursuit of lucre.

Cavorting in muck is not a particularly healthy occupation, and the contemporary American comic hero typically suffers from a variety of symbolic illnesses. Todd Andrews, Humbert Humbert, and Feldman have heart conditions; Stern has a symbolic ulcer; Yossarian, a painful liver; and Portnoy, a complaint. But it is ultimately the humorous society itself that seems most diseased, and the two traditional means of recovering health, religion and medicine, both come under satiric attack. Christianity, which reinforced the comic affirmation in works like Chaucer's *Troilus and Criseyde* and the Miracle and Mystery plays, becomes comically impotent or positively malign. In Heller's novel, for example, God himself seems as ready to use Catch-22 as the next man, prompting Yossarian to label him "a country bumpkin, a clumsy, bungling, brainless, conceited, uncouth hayseed. Good God, how much reverence can you have for a Supreme Being who finds it necessary to include such phenomena as phlegm and tooth decay in His divine system of creation? What in the world was running through that warped, evil, scatological mind of His when He robbed old people of the power to control their bowel movements?"[26] Similarly, Todd Andrews exchanges prayer and God for the warm body of Jane Mack, and Terry Southern's Magic Christian is neither "magic" nor "Christian." Formal religion in the contemporary comic novel is usually ridiculed as an absurd or repressive force.

The medical profession is an even more pervasive source of ridicule. The type of the comic doctor proliferates: Doc Daneeka in *Catch-22*, Dr. Hilarius in *The Crying of Lot 49*, Cap Leech in Hawkes's *The Beetle Leg*, Dr. Bigelow-Martin in *Cabot Wright Begins*, Dr. Marvin Rose in *The Floating Opera*, Dr. Posmanture and "Messy" Massey in Elliott Baker's *A Fine Madness*, the Big Nurse in *One Flew Over the Cuckoo's Nest*, the

Freudian doctors in *Lolita.* Of course, the doctor has traditionally been a stock character of comedy, the most obvious representatives being those of Molière. In *The Mock-Doctor,* for example, when Geronte remarks that "the heart is on the left side, and the liver on the right side," Sganarel observes, "Yes, it was formerly so; but we have altered all that."[27] In *Love's the Best Doctor,* Dr. Bahys insists, "It is better [for a patient] to die according to the rules than to recover contrary to 'em."[28] Doctors in the recent comic novel are similarly humorous. In *Catch-22* the medical response to nearly every complaint is to paint the patient's gums with gentian violet and administer a laxative. Dr. Marvin Rose in *The Floating Opera* gloats over the prospect of getting his hands on a reluctant victim. Dr. Bigelow-Martin in *Cabot Wright Begins,* acting on a theory that America's problem is tiredness caused by too much tension and work, hangs his naked patients from a special hook on his office wall.

Traditionally, the doctor has been depicted as a harmless pedant, the learned crank who pretends to be more than he is. In contemporary fiction he becomes a positive threat. In *A Fine Madness* and *One Flew Over the Cuckoo's Nest,* for example, the doctors have power over life and death, and their solution to the protagonist's "problems" is lobotomy. As symbols of authority, technology, and control, the doctors, like the humor villains, must be rejected through ridicule.

The contemporary comic hero satirically exposes his society, ridiculing its villains and attacking the mechanical and arbitrary assumptions on which it is based. Although the satire thus resembles that of earlier comedy, it has a somewhat different function. As Robert Scholes suggests, "fabulative satire is less certain ethically but more certain esthetically than traditional satire."[29] In traditional satire, laughter is used to reform an aberrant character or society, reestablishing some predetermined social norm. In the contemporary comic novel neither the eccentric character nor the humorous society is reformed through ridicule. Folly is rarely amended. For one thing, the society, which once served as satiric norm, has for the recent comic novelist become almost a satire on itself. Richard Poirier suggests that it is difficult to satirize a Richard Nixon, for example, when he seems so hard at work parodying himself.[30] Humor works by exaggeration, and Nixon, the Machiavellian politician, is in some ways his own exaggeration. In a world grown mechanical and impersonal, where even stupidity, viciousness, and anxiety seem institutionalized, the idea of a social norm is but a further rigidity, a further restriction.

Ultimately, then, the satire is directed not so much against a humorous individual or society as against the absurdity of man's position in the universe. Social aberration is but a fragment of the chaos the novelist perceives in a vast, indifferent cosmos. Although laughter may not reform folly, it does provide a means of facing this cosmic absurdity, imperfection, and indifference. Both hero and society remain unchanged at the end of many contemporary comic novels, but their foibles and failures are seen from a comic perspective that makes them more human, more endurable.

4.

Although the contemporary comic hero rarely converts his humorous society, he is often able to escape it by creating a new one around himself. Although this new society sometimes seems as deluded as the original one, it often embraces the comic values the original society rejected. The characteristic plot pattern of earlier comedy traced a protagonist's growth from self-deception to self-knowledge and maturity. Emma, for example, moves from youthful ignorance to mature wisdom and marries Knightley, the representative of the social norm. Such progress is not possible for the recent comic hero, who is characteristically middle-aged or old, rather than young. Unlike the earlier protagonist whose age often accounted for his folly, the contemporary comic hero has often reached maturity at the outset, and further experience promises no increase in intelligence or wisdom. Todd Andrews, Skipper, Guy Grand, Humbert Humbert, and J. Henry Waugh are all in their fifties, and even younger protagonists like Chief Bromden, rendered deaf and dumb by the Combine's machinations, seem to have been born old.

Therefore, instead of emphasizing integration into society, the typical plot pattern of contemporary comedy focuses escape through artistic creation, a pattern less common in earlier comedy. Aristophanes' Dicaeopolis, who escapes his humorous society by creating a world of peace around himself, and Shakespeare's Prospero, who creates a beautiful pastoral island out of his exile, are two of the very few characters from earlier comedy who reflect this possibility.[31] But even Prospero finally chooses to give up his art and return to Milan. In the recent comic novel, however, escape through art is a central theme.

Images of flying and sailing, for example, proliferate. Kesey's Chief Bromden manages to fly over the cuckoo's nest; Heller's Orr flies his plane into the sea, then rows to freedom in Sweden; Barth's Todd Andrews spends a few hours every day building a boat in his garage. Further, the destination of the voyage out of modern society often takes the form of an imaginary creation, a mythical land. Skipper escapes to his floating island; Pynchon fables an elusive Vheissu; Humbert dreams an island of nymphets; Yossarian and Bromden construct their Sweden and Canada out of their own deep longings for freedom.

Perceiving that language creates "reality," the protagonists try to create new worlds by fictionalizing their experience. Throughout the novels, language has mythical power. In *The Floating Opera* Jane Mack's belly swells up the moment Dr. Marvin Rose says she's pregnant. In *Lolita*, whenever Humbert says something, it becomes fact, his language determining the future. For example, once he's said that he's going to arrive at Lolita's camp in the afternoon, he can't change the arrival time, no matter how hard he tries. Also, when he verbalizes the possibility of Charlotte's death, she promptly dies.

It is thus appropriate that esthetics are more important than ethics in the contemporary comic novel. Since language determines "reality," the form of a novel is crucial, and by becoming an artist, the hero has the best chance of controlling the form of his "reality." Most recent comic heroes are artists of one sort or another. Humbert, Dangerfield, Shillitoe, Portnoy, Rosewater, and Erica Jong's Isadora Wing are poets. Todd Andrews, Skipper, Chief Bromden, and Humbert Humbert write their own fictional biographies, revising their pasts to suit their present needs, actually creating their own history. Cabot Wright becomes "free" at the end of Purdy's novel by seeing his life as a work of art, "all in one piece together like in a movie."[32]

Of course, the protagonists' imaginative creations are rarely as successful or as beautiful as Dicaeopolis' or Prospero's. Todd Andrews cannot escape the fact that he is an impotent old man; Yossarian recognizes that he will probably never get to Sweden; Humbert's and Waugh's created worlds are perhaps as delusive and obsessive as the worlds they seek to escape. Nevertheless, the contemporary comic novelist affirms the effort to create a new world, indeed insists on the moral necessity of doing so. Hawkes, for example, describes the "absolute need to create from the imagination a totally new and necessary fictional landscape or visionary world."[33] Barth observes, "If you are a novelist of a certain type of temperament, then what you really want to do is re-invent the world. . . . What you want to do is re-invent philosophy and the rest—make up your own whole history of the world. Why should it just be Plato and Aristotle? They're nice fellows, but why can't we start over, for variety's sake, and be somebody else instead and have all history go differently?"[34] No matter how deluded or self-deceived the modern comic hero may be, he is also an artist capable of inventing a world.

Thus the contemporary American comic hero is typically a combination of the *eiron* and *alazon* archetypes. Like the conventional *alazon*, the hero unconsciously exposes himself; but like the *eiron*, he satirically exposes his society. Like the conventional *eiron*, the hero is often an artist who creates a world around himself; but like the *alazon*, he usually fails to gain any self-knowledge, remaining deluded to the end. In earlier comedy, the two archetypes were more often kept separate, the conflict between characters structuring the plot. Bottom and Puck, Emma and Knightley, Isabel Archer and Ralph Touchett are examples. Even in *Great Expectations*, where Pip seems to combine the types, Pip's wisdom and artistry are separated in time from his youthful ignorance and egotism. As older narrator, Pip is consistently an *eiron*. As young participant in the action, he is consistently an *alazon*. The modern comic novelist refuses to maintain the neat separation. Unlike Pip, the older narrators are rarely wiser than their younger selves. The fusion is, of course, frustrating for the reader, who has learned to expect growth or self-discovery from the comic protagonist. One theme of the contemporary comic novel may just be the falseness of such conventional expectations.

Perhaps we are now in a position to summarize some of the differences between the contemporary American comic novel and the tradition. First, while sharing the satiric impulses of earlier comedy, the recent comic novel rejects the idea of reformation through ridicule. Instead, laughter reflects a necessary comic perspective on man's position in an absurd universe. Second, the traditional comic types, which were usually separate in earlier comedy, have become inextricably fused, combining fool and wit in a single character. Third, whereas the characteristic plot of earlier comedy traced the integration into a preexistent society, often through marriage, the typical plot of the contemporary comic novel reveals the creation of an imaginative world around the central character, a world that may be obsessive, delusive, and tenuous but that nevertheless affirms survival and comic continuity.

Even these distinctions, of course, must be qualified. The differences are differences of *emphasis*, not kind. The methods, character types, and plot patterns of the contemporary comic novel all derive from similar patterns in earlier comedy. What is new, perhaps, is the combination of types once kept separate and the emphasis on elements once less common.

5.

A perception of the traditional comic conventions operative in the contemporary comic novel is necessary for a full appreciation of one of its characteristic modes—parody. John Barth explains, "If somebody built the Chartres Cathedral now, it would be an embarrassing piece of real estate, wouldn't it? Unless he did it ironically."[35] The recent comic novelist has used parody to build a number of old cathedrals. Barth parodies the eighteenth-century picaresque novel in *The Sot-Weed Factor*; Nabokov parodies literary criticism and eighteenth-century poetry in *Pale Fire*; Hawkes parodies the Western in *The Beetle Leg* and the crime novel in *The Lime Twig*; Bernard Malamud (in *The Natural*) and Coover parody the sports novel; Heller, the epic war novel. The traditional *comic* form most often parodied in the modern comic novel is that of romantic comedy.

In typical romantic comedy, two lovers are opposed by a blocking figure, most often paternal, who disrupts the lovers' union. Usually, the lovers manage to overcome or convert the blocking figure and celebrate their integration into society through their marriage. A number of recent novels parody this pattern. In *The Floating Opera*, for example, the two lovers are Harrison and Jane Mack, and Todd is the blocking figure who disrupts their union. In Barth's parody, however, the lovers virtually *ask* Todd to block their marriage by forming a triad. As in traditional comedy, the Macks finally reject Todd, and they leave the country, recelebrating their union.

Hawkes's *Second Skin* and Nabokov's *Lolita* are structured on similar parodic triads. In *Second Skin*, the parody lovers are

Cassandra and Fernandez, and Skipper is the blocking figure. In *Lolita,* the lovers are Lolita and Quilty, and Humbert is the blocking figure. But in reversals of typical romance, Cassandra and Lolita are trollops, Fernandez and Quilty are perverts, and Skipper and Humbert succeed in disrupting the unions. Further, all three novels are narrated from the point of view of the blocking figure—Todd, Skipper, Humbert—parodying the conventional point of view of the lovers.

In addition to parodying romantic comedy, the contemporary comic novel parodies the picaresque. For instance, whereas the picaresque hero usually seduces a series of women, the modern hero is more often the one seduced. Todd Andrews is seduced by Jane Mack at Todd Point; Skipper is seduced by Miranda in the front seat of her frozen car; Sebastian Dangerfield is seduced by Mary and has to fight her off. In *Lolita,* the hero's seduction by a twelve-year-old is the central joke of the book.

Of course, sex has been a traditional subject for comic treatment. In earlier comedy, the sexual urges and energies reflected in the mythic plot patterns of ritual death and rebirth promised continuity of life. Since parody has the unique capability of simultaneously ridiculing and affirming the form and assumptions of its original, the parody of sexual activity in the recent comic novel simultaneously ridicules and celebrates such notions of continuity. A parody of romantic comedy both ridicules and affirms the assumptions of the form. Parody enables the novelist to hold contradictory impulses in balance. Jorge Luis Borges describes the possibilities in his "Tlon Uqbar, Orbis Tertius." In this imaginary world, "works of fiction contain a single plot, with all its imaginable permutations. Those of a philosophical nature invariably include both the thesis and the antithesis, the rigorous pro and con of a doctrine. A book which does not contain its counterbook is considered incomplete."[36]

Further, by parodying the traditional conventions, the modern comic novelist frustrates the reader's generic expectations, forcing him to revise them. In many recent novels, the ultimate joke is on the reader. By constantly inverting the reader's values and by continually reminding him that fiction is a parody of reality rather than a description of it, the novelist forces the reader to reexamine his assumptions about both literature and life. If the novel is a parody of another literary form, a fiction of a fiction, then perhaps "reality" is itself a fiction. Finally, the parody usually extends to the authors as well, whose self-parody makes fun of their very act of writing. The contemporary comic novelist rarely takes a superior attitude. Instead he exposes his own comic desires for order and reason, reflected in his imposition of artistic form on experience. Thus, character, reader, and author are all intimately involved in the comic exposure.

Parody and self-parody are important features of the recent comic novel, reflecting the stylistic devices typical of comedy: incongruity, surprise, exaggeration, deflation, and repetition. The stylistic device used most frequently is that of setting up an ironic discrepancy between form and content. As L. J. Potts notes, irony is the "exact stylistic equivalent of the comic mode of thought."[37] The contemporary comic novelist typically uses the most refined, polite, lyrical, sophisticated, literary style to recount the most violent, grotesque, or absurd actions. The ironic incongruity between language and action comically reflects the larger incongruities that structure the plot.

Humbert's refined literary language, for example, comically conflicts with the absurdity of his actions. An obsessed pervert and madman, Humbert describes his lechery and lunacy in the language of romance: "Lolita, light of my life, fire of my loins. My sin, my soul. Lo-lee-ta. . . . standing four feet ten in one sock."[38] Later, when Lolita's dress gets stuck in her crotch, Humbert describes "the frock-fold that had stuck in the peach cleft."[39] Finally, after filling Quilty full of bullets in a scene that parodies the obligatory shoot-out from a Western, Humbert labels the mangled victim "a very sick man."[40] Throughout the novel, Humbert tries to conceal the grotesqueness of his subject matter in the poetry of his style.

Similarly, Todd Andrews's sophisticated literary style, with its quaint grace and charm, is incongruous with his professed ignorance of fiction writing and with his scatological subject matter. Todd's major law case, for example, features pickle jars full of feces, and the turning point of the case revolves on a fart. Todd describes the fart in lyrical language:

> But ah, the fart hung heavy in the humid air, long past the lady's flight. It hung, it lolled, it wisped; it miscegenated with the smoke of my cigar, caressed the beading oil on the skin of my nose, lay obscenely on the flat of my desk, among my briefs and papers. It was everywhere, but I had learned, even then, to

> live with nature and my fellow animals. I didn't flinch; I didn't move. Through its dense invisible presence I regarded my oracular wall.[41]

A fart is, perhaps, funny in itself, a comic convention learned in childhood. Certainly the discrepancy between the behavior expected of a proper, decorous young woman and her improper, roisterous farting is funny. But Todd renders it doubly funny by describing the animal function in poetic language. The discrepancy between the act and the actor is comic; the discrepancy between the act and its description is even more comic.

Scatological humor has been a central element of comedy throughout the comic tradition. Chaucer and Swift are obvious examples, but even Henry James names one of his comic characters Fanny Assingham, a joke rivaling Shakespeare's Bottom and William Gaddis's Recktall Brown. In the contemporary comic novel, excrement itself is often central to the plot. In *The Magic Christian*, for example, Guy Grand combines 300 cubic feet of manure, 100 gallons of urine, 50 gallons of blood, and 10,000 $100 bills in a large cauldron, lights a fire underneath it, and watches the people scurry. The plot of *The Crying of Lot 49* depends on a message written on the wall of a latrine, and the turning points of both *The Ginger Man* and Edward Lewis Wallant's *The Tenants of Moonbloom* occur when a swollen bathroom wall bursts, covering the characters with excrement.

The scatological humor serves two comic purposes. Balancing the imagery of art and artistic creation mentioned earlier, it reminds both character and reader of their animal nature. While Todd Andrews, for example, wants to believe that his life is governed by creative intelligence and reason, it is clearly governed as much by bodily process and accident. It is a fart, after all, not logic or intelligence, that saves his law case. Second, the scatological humor seems a comment on the modern obsession with cleanliness. Dangerfield's unwashed eloquence, for example, ridicules by contrast the sterile cleanliness demanded by his society.

Noting the emphasis on excrement and violence, on death and the grotesque, on the disintegration of social institutions and the erosion of traditional values, some critics have concluded that the recent comic novel is more extreme than its predecessors. Indeed, the obvious strain and tension under the surface of contemporary comedy might suggest an affinity with the tragic as well as the comic. But it is wrong to assume that death, pain, and violence are outside the traditional province of comedy. W. C. Fields explains, "I never saw anything funny that wasn't terrible. If it causes pain, it's funny; if it doesn't, it isn't."[42] Wylie Sypher traces the comic violence of modern literature back to its origins. "In fact, to interpret the complications and contradictions in comedy, we must look far backward toward Aristotle and the Greeks; for the meanings in comedy are tribally old, and Bergson and Meredith refine almost beyond recognition the primitive violence of comedy, which, curiously, reappears again in James, Kafka, and 'us moderns.'"[43] Strong, dark laughter has been a primary element in most great comedy. The recent comic novel is certainly no more extreme in its humor that Swift's proposal that babies be eaten, Shakespeare's depiction of Caliban, or Chaucer's cloacal jokes in "The Miller's Tale." Walter Kerr concludes, "Comedy at its most penetrating derives from what we normally regard as tragic."[44] It is not the subject matter but the author's attitude toward it that determines the tragic or comic basis of a literary form.

John Hawkes describes the comic attitude toward pain and violence:

> This constant is a quality of coldness, detachment, ruthless determination to face up to the enormities of ugliness and potential violence within ourselves and in the world around us, and to bring to this exposure a savage or saving comic spirit and the saving beauties of language. The need is to maintain the truth of the fractured picture; to expose, ridicule, attack, but always to create and to throw into new light our potential for violence and absurdity as well as for graceful action.[45]

That the comic spirit is "saving" as well as "savage," affirming the potential for "graceful action," is evident in the endings of many contemporary comic novels. Far from reflecting despair or hopelessness, as is sometimes claimed, the endings often reflect ingredients typical of the comic form. Todd Andrews lives on to write a novel, reinventing his past; Skipper creates a pastoral island society based on love and compassion; Stern confronts the kike man and then lovingly embraces his wife and child; Shillitoe finds a haven with Rhoda in Cob City, Indiana, and finishes his poem; Rosewater adopts fifty-seven children and tells them to "be fruitful and multiply"; Orr escapes to Sweden, and Yossarian prepares to follow; Bromden leaves a shrunken institution and returns to his native village; Dangerfield embraces Mary during the Christmas season, in a parody of the Christian myth. While the endings clearly qualify any conventional notions of "happiness," they do not reflect nihilism or despair.

6.

The contemporary American comic novel thus takes its place within a recognizable comic tradition, combining the conventional character types, plot patterns, and stylistic devices of earlier comedy. Being comic in form, it by definition affirms certain comic norms and values. L. J. Potts observes, "All comic writers must have a norm in view."[46] Robert Corrigan agrees, "If there are no generally held social norms, then there can be no great comedy. The break *from* the norm has no meaning unless there is a commonly held norm from which to break."[47] Comedy depends for its effect on the perception of discrepancies between conflicting values. Humor cannot exist unless the audience is capable of perceiving incongruity. Deviation, foolishness, stupidity, and ignorance are not funny unless there are standards of normalcy, intelligence, and knowledge by which to judge them. The writer of comedy assumes the existence of such norms or standards by the very act of writing.

One difference between earlier comedy and the recent comic novel, however, is that while norms and values formerly existed within the work itself, they now exist outside the work. Contemporary comedy has no Knightley or Highbury to symbolize the norm by which the protagonist is measured. Walter Kerr describes the situation in reference to modern comic drama: "The only way in which the play can be regarded as funny is by comparison *with something that is not present in the play.* Outside the play, hovering over it like a race memory, is a set of affirmations formerly believed in. . . . The play *as a whole* will seem funny in proportion as we bring to the theater with us a habit of seeing life in terms of ancient aspirations."[48] The "ancient aspirations" that the contemporary comic novelist relies upon are the typical norms of comedy: love, peace, goodness, compassion, intelligence, the value of life itself. The comic writer tries to meet the terrors of an absurd world with a "savage or saving comic spirit" in an effort to defend and celebrate these permanent human values.

Traditional comic theory is only partially successful in describing the contemporary comic novel. George Meredith's emphasis on intellectual wit and satire and his description of the comic spirit as "humanely malign" clearly pertain to recent comedy. But the contemporary comic writer neither shares Meredith's view of laughter as a social corrective nor believes in the possibility of reforming folly through ridicule. The didactic impulses of Meredith's theory no longer apply.

Similarly, the Freudian theory of comedy as a means for overcoming social and psychological repression by liberating the id from the superego is only partially appropriate. While the recent comic novel continues to attack repression and restraint, ridiculing whatever is mechanical or sterile, the old Puritan anxieties that inform Freud's theory have, for the most part, been overcome. Puritan repression seems as antiquated an idea as that of the social norm.

The contemporary comic novel characteristically focuses on the metaphysical, rather than the social or psychological, problems of mankind. Robert Scholes observes, "The Black Humorist is not concerned with what to do about life but with how to take it. In this respect Black Humor has certain affinities with some existentialist attitudes."[49] The existentialist vision of man poised on the brink of the absurd, ridiculously refusing to admit the ultimate triumph of death and destruction and learning to laugh at the discrepancy between his desire for meaning and the indifference of the universe, is essentially comic. Wylie Sypher argues that the perception of the absurd itself guarantees a kind of comic humanism. "As long as man is aware of his existence as being absurd, thwarted, blocked, or irrelevant, a variety of humanism persists, simply through man's awareness of his plight. . . . To be conscious of the meaninglessness is to have a metaphysical position that is privileged."[50] The contemporary American comic novel struggles to face the void without flinching, to endure the absurd, and, by viewing life from a comic perspective, to enjoy the endurance.

Some critics worry that the replacement of social norms and Puritan repressions, two important sources of earlier comedy, with the existential absurd, may threaten comedy's (and the novel's) very existence. When all illusions are shattered, and man is left staring into the abyss, can any attitude prevail other than despair? But in the continuing debate over the death of the novel, the future of comedy, and the meaninglessness of modern life, the novelists themselves seem determined to have the last laugh. And it won't be their last.

The chapters that follow attempt to document, by generic description and close analysis of five representative texts, the general observations made in this introduction. Admittedly, the choice of specific works for extended analysis is somewhat arbitrary. Any number of recent novels could have been included: Pynchon's *The Crying of Lot 49* or *V*, Donleavy's *The Ginger Man*, Heller's *Catch-22*, Wallant's *The Tenants of Moonbloom*, Friedman's *Stern*, Baker's *A Fine Madness*, Vonnegut's *God Bless You, Mr. Rosewater*, Elkin's *A Bad Man*, and Bellow's *Herzog* are obvious candidates. But the five novels examined here seem peculiarly representative of the kind of comedy that characterizes the contemporary American novel, a comedy that has been largely misinterpreted or disregarded by critics. Taken as a group, these five books reveal remarkable similarities of style, tone, character, plot, structure, and world view that typically define the recent comic novel.

Further, the five novels included here embody five central themes or metaphors for America that have recurred in much contemporary American comic fiction. In *The Floating Opera*, John Barth personifies America in Todd Andrews, an artist-hero who rewrites his own personal history and that of twentieth-century America as well. In *Second Skin*, John Hawkes examines the effects of militarism and violence on twentieth-century American life; Skipper is a retired naval officer faced with a world that seems to be, on both the public and the private level, constantly at war. In *Lolita*, Vladimir Nabokov parodies America as the sum of its goods, a society in which a romanticized consumerism is the ultimate value. In *One Flew Over the Cuckoo's Nest*, Ken Kesey sees America in terms of the institution, a repressive bureaucracy dedicated to stifling the individual. In *The Universal Baseball Association*, Robert Coover uses a sports metaphor to examine American life and to provide an apocalyptic glimpse of the future.

Thus, the five chapters that follow move thematically from an examination of twentieth-century American history, through militarism, consumerism, the institution, and sports, to an apocalyptic view of the future. Further, the arrangement of the chapters is loosely chronological, reflecting the novels' historical focuses. *The Floating Opera* focuses the period from 1900 to 1950; *Second Skin* focuses the immediate post-World War II period; *Lolita* focuses the fifties; *One Flew Over the Cuckoo's Nest* focuses the sixties; *The Universal Baseball Association* focuses the late sixties and beyond.

Finally, considered together these novels reflect the various kinds of comic affirmation typical of contemporary American fiction. Todd Andrews absurdly affirms life over death by relying on his intelligence, his ironic wit, and comic artistry, while, like Meredith's Comic Spirit, anesthetizing his heart. Skipper, in some ways Todd's opposite, relies on his heart, not his head, using his unbounded compassion and wise love to create an alternative reality. Humbert Humbert tries to combine both Todd's intellectual wit and Skipper's wisdom of the heart. Although Humbert dies, paralleling the usual expulsion of the blocking figure in traditional comedy, the reader lives on, himself becoming the butt of Nabokov's joke and the promise of life's continuity. If Humbert fails to combine head and heart, absurdly fooling himself and the reader, McMurphy succeeds, restoring both the emotional and intellectual life of the inmates in the institution and teaching them how to laugh. Finally, J. Henry Waugh is in some ways a combination of all the other protagonists. Like Todd, he is able to expose the foolishness of his humorous society, regarding it with a detached ironic eye. Like Skipper, he has a great fund of love and compassion, if not for "real" people, then for the denizens of his imagined universe. Like Humbert, he is obsessed with what may be a delusion, but like Bromden he manages to escape a repressive reality by disappearing. The combination of possibilities within Waugh enables Coover to speculate philosophically on the themes introduced by the other authors. Thus, these five novels represent the typical modes of comic affirmation: detachment, irony, and wit; love, humor, and compassion; expulsion, parody, and balance; laughter, satire, and escape through artistic creation.

The introductory overview, coupled with the generic analysis of representative texts, should reveal the relationship of the contemporary American comic novel to earlier comic literature, illuminate the authors' affirmative themes and concerns, focus the necessary ambivalence of the protagonists, provide practical models for approaching other comic novels not included here, and perhaps throw a few pies, too.

II.

Dwarfed into Dignity
John Barth's The Floating Opera

Early in John Barth's *The Floating Opera,* Todd Andrews warns the reader that he is

> less than consistent in practically everything, so that any general statement about me will probably be inadequate. To be sure, many people make such statements anyway—I get the impression at times that doing so constitutes a chief activity of the town's idle intelligences—but I have the not-inconsiderable satisfaction of knowing that they're wrong and of hearing them contradict one another (and thereby, I conclude, cancel one another out).[1]

In a sense Todd is talking to the critics, who have obligingly contradicted one another since 1956, when the novel was first published. Todd Andrews has been seen both as an existential hero and as a nihilistic fraud, and Barth's attitude has been labeled both affirmative and perverse. Campbell Tatham, for example, observes that Todd's "clear and impressive ability to manipulate point of view demonstrates in itself a realm in which order and meaning are apparently inherent,"[2] while Stanley Edgar Hyman insists that Todd is a "victim of his Oedipus complex, a latent homosexual, a cold fish, and a malicious sadist."[3] John C. Stubbs argues that Barth "goes past the nihilistic refutation of absolute value to an affirmation of relative value,"[4] while W. L. Godshalk concludes that Barth's "world" is a "hopeless" one "where, ultimately, nothing is of value."[5]

The critical response is further complicated by the fact that Barth wrote rather different endings to the two editions of the book. The "happy ending" to the 1956 edition was apparently a revision required by Barth's editor; the less happy ending to the 1967 edition is apparently the original one. In the 1956 edition Todd fails to commit suicide, feeling spontaneous emotion for Jeanine Mack and excitedly affirming the viability of relative values. In the 1967 edition Todd also fails to commit suicide, but feels no emotion and affirms no values. While readers of the 1956 edition tended to view Todd affirmatively, readers of the 1967 edition have tended to view him more negatively. Todd

Andrews would be delighted with the critical contradictions.

The one point that most critics have agreed upon, however, is that *The Floating Opera* is a *comic* novel. Barth himself observed that the novel is a "nihilistic comedy."[6] But most critics, while noting the comedy, emphasize the novel's nihilism, the unreliability of its narrator, or its existential backdrop, without describing the novel's comic form or the comic tradition to which its hero belongs. Nevertheless, generic description is a necessary prerequisite of an understanding of Todd's role in the novel and Barth's attitude toward him. *The Floating Opera* belongs to an observable comic tradition, combining several types of conventional comic character and plot.[7] In some ways Todd Andrews is both an *eiron* and an *alazon*, and the plot moves toward both integration and exposure.

The Floating Opera is a comic novel about a man writing a comic novel about his own past. The hero of Todd Andrews's comic novel is clearly meant to be the traditional self-deprecator and artist, the comic spirit who humorously criticizes his ridiculous society with the object of improving it and of understanding himself more clearly. From the outset Todd presents himself as the plain dealer, a man of common sense and reason who will make up for his lack of sophistication as a fiction writer by telling his story just as simply and clearly as possible. Since he is a beginning novelist and has no talent, he will treat the reader as solicitously as a guest, explaining everything in a pleasant and friendly way, making no effort to confuse or mystify. In the first few paragraphs Todd establishes his friendly relationship with the reader:

> I intend directly to introduce myself, caution you against certain possible interpretations of my name, explain the significance of this book's title, and do several other gracious things for you, like a host fussing over a guest, to make you as comfortable as possible and to dunk you gently into the meandering stream of my story. (2)

Later in the first chapter Todd repeats his decision to be a plain dealer. "I think that what I shall do is try not to comment at all, but simply stick to the facts" (6). Throughout the novel, Todd maintains the role of plain dealer and self-deprecator, particularly about his lack of skill as a writer. Early in the book he exclaims, "Good heavens, how does one write a novel! . . . I see already that storytelling isn't my cup of tea" (2). Later he insists, "My prose is a plodding, graceless thing, and I've no comprehension of stylistic tricks" (168).

Despite his protestations of ignorance, however, it is immediately apparent that Todd knows a great deal about fiction writing. Like the *eiron* of conventional comedy, Todd pretends ignorance while demonstrating his extensive knowledge. While claiming to know nothing about story writing, he demonstrates his mastery of narrative technique and stylistic tricks. He's aware of the literary convention of beginning a story *in medias res*, and he explains that he won't subject the reader to that—he'll tune his piano first (2). By the fourth paragraph he has shown his control of at least one stylistic trick by establishing four related patterns of metaphor: the introduction is piano tuning; the author is a host, and the reader is his guest; the story is a meandering stream; digressions are fox hunts. The whole novel is, of course, structured on the "Floating Opera" metaphor. Further, in Chapter 3, entitled "Coitus," Todd admits that he knows something about "climaxes," an important element of any story, and one of numerous clever puns that recur throughout the book (18). Chapter 20, in which Todd confesses his ignorance of stylistic tricks, begins with the most obvious stylistic trick in the book: two parallel and simultaneous introductions.

The role that Todd Andrews creates for himself in *The Floating Opera* is thus that of the *eiron*, the self-deprecator who pretends ignorance but knows a great deal. Further, like the typical *eiron*, Todd functions as a comic spirit, laughing at the humorous delusions and expectations of the less sensitive members of his society. Meredith's description of the comic spirit reflects this aspect of Todd. When people "offend sound reason, fair justice; are false in humility or mined with conceit, in the individual or in the bulk—the spirit overhead will look humanely malign and cast an oblique light on them, followed by volleys of silvery laughter."[8] As a wise, alert, ironical demon of the upper air, criticizing folly and stupidity, Todd laughs first at the reader himself. Knowing that a reader conventionally (and irrationally) expects certain things of a novel, Todd delights in frustrating those expectations. For example, after tricking the reader into trusting him, promising to stick to the facts and to be the reader's friend, Todd wanders from the facts, even refusing to verify the single most important fact of the story—the exact day on which it takes place. After years of research, collecting peach baskets full of material about the day in 1937 when he didn't commit suicide, Todd has neglected to determine whether it was June 21 or 22 (22 or 23 in the 1956 edition). Todd knows that he could easily verify the date. He could check his files to see when he settled the Butler–Morton case; he could check Dr. Rose's records to see when he had his unusual checkup; he could check the newspaper to see when the "Opera" was in town. But Todd delights in frustrating the reader's expectations, and he refers continually to the uncertainty of the date.

In Chapter 9 he directs another joke at the reader's conventional expectations. As he opens his morning's mail, the nineteenth-century comic convention of secret or lost letters is doubled and redoubled. Todd gets Jane Mack's answer to a note he had sent her about Capt. Osborn:

> Darling, if you hoped in some way to hurt me again with your note this morning, you failed. I'm not disturbed at all. I will do exactly what you suggest, my dear, if you will see Marvin Rose for a complete physical, to find out why you're such a pansy. Love, Jane. (74)

Of course, Todd has not told the reader what he asked Jane to do in his note, and her response remains mysterious. Todd then gets a letter from Eustacia Callader that he knows may be crucial to the Mack law case, but he sets it aside without opening it while he reads the "Floating Opera" handbill that had lain forgotten in his pocket all morning. Over thirty pages later in the novel, Todd finally reads the important letter from Eustacia. He remarks, "It could contain anything from nonsense to the key to three million dollars, and it was merely as a disciplinary exercise that I'd postponed reading it until after I'd read the other letters and the handbill, and had called Marvin Rose. But I shan't exact such discipline from you, reader" (105). The joke is, of course, that Todd has exacted just such discipline from the reader, making him wait for the contents of the handbill, his note to Jane, and the letter from Eustacia. A few chapters later Todd again jokes about the reader's voyeuristic role: "Are you so curious as to follow me down the hall to the men's room?" (149). As comic spirit, Todd thus laughs at the reader's conventional expectations.

But Todd doesn't laugh only at the reader; he seems to have the ability to see the joke in nearly everything. For example, he appreciates the humor of nature's "heavy-handed symbolizing." When he sees two dogs copulating in front of a funeral parlor, he complains that nature "seems at times fairly to club one over the head with significances such as this clumsy 'life-in-the-face-of-death' scenario, so obvious that it was embarrassing. One is constantly being confronted with a sun that bursts from behind the clouds just as the home team takes the ball; ominous rumblings of thunder when one is brooding desultorily at home" (106–7). Todd self-consciously ends his own novel brooding desultorily at home while an "absurd thunderstorm . . . broke all around" (247).

Todd also perceives the comic discrepancy between man's human and animal natures. He laughs at "fucking dogs" and "doubler crabs" because they remind him of himself as a clumsy and inexperienced adolescent trying to make love to Betty June Gunter. "Nothing, to me, is so consistently, profoundly, earth-shakingly funny as we animals in the act of mating. Reader, if you are young and would live on love; if in the flights of intercourse you feel that you and your beloved are models for a Phidias—then don't include among the trappings of your love-nest a good plate mirror. For a mirror can reflect only what it sees, and what it sees is funny" (121). *The Floating Opera* is in part a mirror held up to show the discrepancy between the ideal and the real.

Todd also finds fun in the manners and forms of his society. His law cases, based as they are on timely farts and pickled feces, expose the humorous aspects of social interaction. Todd treats the law, the respected symbol of justice and order, as a game. Perceiving that justice is based more on whim and emotion than on reason, Todd enjoys its intricacies and incongruities. To win his case for Harrison Mack, Todd has to prove that Harrison has "kept clear of communist sympathy" since 1932. Todd knows that Harrison's contributions to the Spanish loyalists (who are supported by the communists) don't logically make him sympathetic to communism, since that conclusion is based on a faulty enthymeme, but he also knows that logic isn't very important in winning a case. When his opponent calls Harrison a "blue blood with a Red heart" Todd knows that his case is lost. "How could mere justice cope with poetry?" (92). Todd realizes that the law itself is an elaborate fiction-making process whereby language is used to create the "truth." The skillful orator has the best chance of creating a winning fiction.

Todd appreciates the humor of the situation even if Harrison, who stands to lose three million dollars, doesn't. When Harrison adopts the role of pathetic victim, lamenting the loss of his money, Todd, in his role as comic spirit, jibes at him, "You're wallowing, Harrison. It's swinish. . . . We act as if we could choose, and so we can, in effect. All you have to do to be strong is stop being weak" (97). Todd's ridicule reforms Harrison who, by the end, is strong enough not to value the money.

Similarly, Todd provokes Mr. Haecker to examine his self-delusions about enjoying old age. When Mr. Haecker insists in a cliché-ridden speech that "intellectual discussion, after all, is the real joy of the winter of life, when other pleasures have flown, as it were," Todd laughs malignly. "You know very well it's an act. What the hell's glorious about your old age? What's wrong with facing the fact that things are pretty bleak, and complaining like hell about it?" (161). Mr. Haecker's response to Todd's laughter is inadequate, and he tries to commit suicide, complete with black robe, candles, and an annotated copy of *Hamlet*. His suicide is, of course, like Todd's, comically interrupted.

Todd, then, like the comic spirit, laughs at the folly of his society. The situation in which he seems most "humanely malign" is the sexual triad involving himself and the Macks. The triad, a comic convention Barth has used in subsequent novels, appears throughout comic literature. In conventional comedy, when two men love the same woman the natural order is upset and comedy results. This convention is evident in Shakespearean comedy, for example, when the hero and heroine, blocked from union throughout the play, marry at the end. The Mack–Todd triad is partly a parody of this typical comic situation, since the Macks *ask* Todd to block their marriage, humorously inviting him to participate in it. Todd, astounded at his good fortune, is only too happy to oblige them, while satirically undermining their experiment. Jane explains their position logically, carefully ignoring any emotional implications:

> "We talked it over," she explained, embarrassed again. "Harrison thinks the world of you, and I do, too. We don't see why a woman can't make love to somebody she likes a lot, just for the pleasure of it, without a lot of complications. Do you?"
>
> "Of course not," I said quickly.
>
> "That's how we felt," she said. I was becoming curious and a bit amused. "Harrison and I love each other completely," Jane went on, speaking very solemnly and scratching a fly bite on

> one leg. "So much that neither of us could possibly ever be jealous. If you thought for a minute that I didn't love him because of what I've done, I'd die."
>
> "Nonsense," I assured her, just as solemnly. "I understand everything." (27)

Todd's witty perception of the Macks' foolishness is apparent from the beginning. Jane's solemn rationality, Todd's mock solemnity and amusement, the fly bite on Jane's leg, all gently undercut the Macks' deluded reliance on reason over emotion. It seems clear to Todd that the relationship is doomed to failure.

From the outset, the Macks expose their own foolishness. When Harrison arrives, Todd perceives that he wants Todd to feel obligated to him for his gift of Jane. "*Don't feel obligated!*" Harrison insists repeatedly. "It's like playing tennis" (30). Todd assures Harrison he feels no obligation. Later Harrison argues, in a humorous tangle of logic and rationalization, "A woman can love two or several men in the same way at the same time . . . or in different ways at the same time, or in the same way at different times, or in different ways at different times" (34).

Todd is not content, however, to let the Macks expose themselves. As comic spirit, he punctures their pretensions. Realizing that Harrison wants some payment in return for Jane's favors, Todd lies that she was his first sexual experience (31). Harrison is delighted. Later, however, Todd casually corrects his first lie with a second, implying a sexual relationship with his black client, Dorothy Miner. Harrison is shocked racially and morally, thus undermining his pretense of being a liberal thinker (39).

The triad is ridiculed not only by verbal undercutting, but by a structural doubling as well. When Capt. Osborn admits to Todd that he has listened in on Todd's and Jane's lovemaking, Todd gets an idea. He proposes to Jane that she allow Osborn to see her naked, and she agrees on the condition that Todd get a physical examination from Dr. Marvin Rose. The triad Todd proposes comically doubles that of himself and the Macks. Like Todd, Capt. Osborn is cast in the role of uninvolved participant, but the eighty-three-year-old retired oyster dredger feels more excitement and emotion than the young lovers. Jane herself sees the humor in Todd's proposal and refuses to take him seriously.

The Mack–Todd triad is then redoubled comically toward the end of the novel. Todd gives his five-thousand-dollar inheritance from his father to Colonel Morton, proprietor of Morton's Marvelous Tomatoes, Inc. Like Harrison Mack before him, Todd insists that "it's a gift," repeatedly assuring Morton that he should feel "no obligation." The episode climaxes when Todd, drunk at the Mortons' New Year's Eve party, finds himself in the shower dancing with Mrs. Morton under the watchful eye of the Colonel, who has finally managed to settle his obligation.

The comic doubling of the central triad serves to ridicule the assumptions on which the triad is based. The painful lesson the Macks learn is that reason can't be imposed on sex and love. Having been the butt of their own joke, the Macks finally perceive the absurdity, and recelebrate their marriage by leaving Todd and traveling in Italy.

In his role as comic spirit, Todd laughs at the pretensions and delusions of his society. But he also laughs at himself, attaining some painful self-knowledge. The whole book is predicated on Todd's discovery of his penchant for avoiding the truth by donning masks, assuming roles.

> My heart, reader! My heart! You must comprehend quickly, if you are to comprehend at all, that those masks were not assumed to hide my face, but to hide my heart from my mind, and my mind from my heart. Understand it now, because I may not live to end the chapter! To be sure, each mask hid other things as well, as a falseface hides identity and personality as well as nose and mouth; but it was to hide my enigmatic heart that I became a rake, a saint, and then a cynic. (219)

Todd confesses that for much of his life he has avoided the central question symbolized by his heart condition—death. His subacute bacteriological endocarditis with a special complication toward myocardial infarction means that "any day I may fall quickly dead" (5). To avoid the question of death, Todd has donned a series of masks. After his first sexual encounter with Betty June Gunter, when he caught sight of himself in the mirror and laughed hysterically at the sight of copulation, Todd became a rake. Later, as a result of his second experience with Betty June, in which he was almost killed and suffered an attack of his prostate infection, Todd became a saint. Then, as a result of his father's suicide in 1930, Todd became a cynic. So, from 1917 to 1937 Todd passed through three attitudes: the hedonism of the rake, the renunciation of the saint, and the disenchantment of the cynic. On the night before June 21 or 22, 1937, the last of Todd's masks falls away, and he is left facing the ultimate question of suicide. It occurs to Todd that the only way to assert his control over his heart, the only way to demonstrate his freedom, is to kill himself. The discovery is chilling. "I heard beyond it the whistle of the black winds of Chaos; my hackles rose, as if I had been breathed upon by a cold sigh from the pit" (201). Faced with the problems of a valueless universe and suicide, however, Todd finally and absurdly chooses life. Like the typical comic hero, he progresses from self-deception through a ritual death to a kind of self-awareness that enables him to live. This should be no surprise in a novel in which the protagonist has been confronting imminent death and asserting life from the very beginning. Early in the book Todd explains that he pays his hotel bill one day at a time as a reminder of the futility of long-range plans, given his heart condition. On the other hand, Todd has been following a long-range plan for most of his life, his interminable *Inquiry*. "I begin each day with a gesture of cynicism, and close it with a gesture of faith; or, if you prefer, begin it by reminding myself that, for me at least, goals and objectives are without value, and close it by demonstrating that the fact is irrelevant. A gesture of temporality, a gesture of eternity. It is in the tension between these two gestures that I have lived my adult life" (50). With this understanding of his situation, Todd is able to view even his death from a comic perspective. "Having heard tick, will I hear tock? Having served, will I volley? Having sugared, will I cream? Itching, will I scratch? Hemming, will I haw?" (49).

In many ways, then, Todd resembles the *eiron* of conventional comedy. Self-deprecator and artist, he plays the role of comic spirit, laughing at the absurdities of his society and himself. This is the view Todd would like the reader to accept, and the 1956 ending especially seems to affirm it. But Barth does not leave the situation so simple. It is clear, particularly in the 1967 edition, that while Todd is in many ways an *eiron*, he is also an *alazon*, a boastful impostor and fool.

Throughout the book he exposes negative aspects of himself of which he seems unaware. For example, in his role as *eiron* Todd constantly deprecates himself, but he has a knack for turning self-deprecation into a boast. Early in the book Todd catalogues all of his inadequacies:

> But my talent for doing correctly the small things that constitute the glorious whole was defective—I never mastered first

> principles—and so the finished product, while perhaps impressive to the untutored, was always mediocre to the knowledged. To how many of my young achievements does this not apply! I dazzled old ladies at piano recitals, but never really mastered the scales; won the tennis championship of my high school—a school indifferent to tennis—but never really mastered the strokes; graduated first in my class, but never really learned to think. And so on: it's a painful list. (59)

On the surface Todd seems to be criticizing himself. But examined closely, the boast in this subtle confession is clear. Todd insists that even though he never mastered the basics he was first in his class, delighted everyone, and succeeded marvelously without even trying. What he's ultimately claiming is that he's a natural-born genius. Even though he was no good at anything, he was much better than anyone else. He claims to be confessing inadequacy, but he's really boasting superiority.

Later in the book he exposes himself similarly. He says he is the "best lawyer on the Eastern shore" and then qualifies the statement because he's afraid the reader will interpret it as self-praise.

> If I thought the practice of law absolutely important, then my statement would indeed be as much a boast as a description; but truthfully I consider advocacy, jurisprudence, even justice, to have no more intrinsic importance than, say, oyster-shucking. And you'd understand, wouldn't you, that if a man like myself asserted with a smile that he was the peninsula's best oyster shucker (I'm not), or cigarette roller, or pinball-machine tilter, he'd not be guilty of prideful boasting? (71)

Here Todd boasts that he's the best lawyer but argues it isn't a boast because he doesn't value the profession. "A man like myself," a superior man, wouldn't value anything as plebeian as law. Again, he's the natural-born genius, the best at everything, even though he doesn't think it important. Todd's self-deprecations are thus often boasts in disguise, aligning him with the comic fool or impostor.

Throughout the novel, Todd contradicts himself in ways he doesn't suspect. He claims that since there are no absolute values, there is no reason to get excited about anything. He insists that he is "thorough but unenthusiastic" (100). But on the very page on which he makes this claim he uses four exclamation marks, indicating his enthusiasm for the Mack law case. When Mrs. Lake farts soon thereafter he cries "By God now!" and "rushes" out to see her, obviously displaying more than intellectual indifference. Also, when Jane Mack first surprises him in bed he is so excited and enthusiastic that he ejaculates prematurely. Todd does not maintain the calm, rational indifference he claims.

He contradicts himself in more fundamental ways as well. Todd says that as a result of his war experience he was cured of several things. "I seldom daydream any more, even for an instant. I never expect very much from myself or my fellow animals. I almost never characterize people in a word or phrase, and rarely pass judgment on them at all. I no longer look for the esteem or approbation of my acquaintances. I do things more slowly, more systematically, and more thoroughly" (67). Todd's list of things he doesn't do reads more like a catalogue of things he does do. He has a staring wall in his office to which he devotes a considerable amount of time daydreaming. When Harrison Mack grows despondent at the thought of losing three million dollars, Todd expects him to be strong to the point of accepting a kind of "catch-22." If the money is important to Harrison, Todd won't help him win it. But if the money is not important, then Todd will help him. Todd characterizes both himself and Harrison repeatedly in "a word or phrase" as a rake, a saint, or a cynic. Todd also continually asks the reader for support, looking for his esteem. When Todd explains the Betty June affair to the reader, for example, he pleads, "Don't you agree that this is probably how it was?" (139). Finally, he decides to commit suicide on but a moment's consideration, failing to proceed "slowly, systematically, thoroughly" in what is the most important decision of his life. Todd's unconscious contradictions comically backfire on him.

Further, while Todd is in some ways a comic spirit, ridiculing the Macks for letting their reason get astride of their emotions, Barth also casts Todd in the role of blocking figure and refuser of festivity, a role usually played by the *alazon*. As I noted earlier, the Mack–Todd triad is a parody of traditional romantic comedy. Romantic comedy usually presents two lovers who are blocked by a figure of authority. The audience sympathizes with the lovers, and after some kind of ritual death the lovers triumph, either by defeating the blocking figure and expelling him from society or by converting him and thus incorporating him into a new society. Barth parodies this convention by having the lovers request a blocking figure and by presenting the drama not from the point of view of the lovers as in typical comedy, but from the point of view of the blocking figure, Todd. As blocking figure, Todd is doomed from the start by the conventions of comedy. He is forced to play the refuser of festivity, lying to the Macks, meanly insinuating that Jeanine is his daughter, not Harrison's (145), and disrupting their marriage. In the end, the Macks, like lovers in a traditional romantic comedy, escape Todd and recelebrate their marriage. From the blocking figure's point of view this could be tragic, but Todd manages to do what the Macks can't: remain unemotionally detached. What Todd never realizes is that the lesson he has taught the Macks, that reason alone is not enough on which to base a life, is a lesson he himself hasn't learned. Todd's criticism of the Macks comically reverses on him. Nevertheless, with comic resiliency he rebounds from the affair determined to continue living.

Similarly, Todd's criticism of Mr. Haecker's false optimism turns back on him. Barth is very careful to establish Mr. Haecker as Todd's comic double. When Todd has his conversation with Haecker midway through the book, Haecker is "taut as a piano wire," and Todd notes that he is "tuning his piano," paralleling Todd's own practice in beginning his novel (158–59). Haecker's smile, "thin and broken like the smiles of army recruits hearing heavy artillery for the first time," recalls Todd's army experience and reminds Todd of a sick smile he once gave his father. Like Todd, Haecker has a "wardrobe of masks," and he keeps a thirteen-volume diary that corresponds to Todd's own *Inquiry*. Early in the book Todd notes that June 21 or 22 "was going to be as momentous a day for him [Haecker] as for me" (42), and Haecker's melodramatic suicide attempt at the end comically parodies Todd's. Todd would like to ally himself with Capt. Osborn, who rages against death; the reader realizes that he is comically doubled by Haecker. When he criticizes Haecker for his absurd philosophy, Todd is thus unconsciously criticizing himself as well. For Haecker finally articulates the position at which Todd himself arrives. "One is finally able to live in the company of his thoughts. . . . But *you* certainly must be aware that the life of solitary contemplation is the best—after all, you're alone, too" (162). From 1937 on Todd lives in the company of his thoughts, writing an "autobiographical" book.

As Todd's double, Mr. Haecker parodies Todd's movement toward an abortive suicide. Todd's movement toward suicide is also parodied by the show on board the "Floating Opera" at the end. Just as Shakespeare's rustics parody the central action of *A Midsummer Night's Dream* by performing "Pyramus and Thisbe," so Captain Adam's minstrel show parodies the action of *The Floating Opera.* The shows begins with T. Wallace Whitaker's rendition of a scene from *As You Like It* that reflects Todd's masks: "All the world's a stage . . . and one man in his time plays many parts." Then Whitaker ridiculously and ineptly recites Hamlet's soliloquy, parodying Todd's own "philosophical" approach to suicide. Later, Sweet Sally Starbuck sings a series of songs that further comment on the action of the novel—"Beautiful Dreamer," "Just a Song at Twilight," and "It's a Sin to Tell a Lie"—songs appropriate to a novel in which the protagonist dreams of a perfect woman, contemplates death, and lies to his friends and himself. The final act, in which Burley Joe Wells mimes "The Great Steamboat Explosion," comically doubles Todd's own plans to blow up the "Floating Opera."

Todd's whole philosophical quest is effectively ridiculed by parodic doubling. Barth's criticism of Todd is focused most clearly, however, in Todd's account of his five emotional experiences. As I noted earlier, Todd attains a measure of self-awareness when he realizes that he has been adopting masks to hide the fact of death. What Todd doesn't realize is that the masks also hide his emotions. Todd's diseased heart may be symbolic of his death, as Todd notes, but it may also be symbolic of his diseased emotions. Todd's heart trouble may refer to his inability to love or feel normal human emotions. Similarly his name, which is almost the German *tod,* or "death," could indicate that the novel is about an "almost death" as Todd claims, or it could suggest that Todd himself is almost dead emotionally.

As with the Macks and Mr. Haecker, whom Todd criticizes, Todd's problem seems to be a tendency to assert reason over emotion. Toward the end of the novel he confesses his "last secret":

> In my life I have experienced emotion intensely on only five occasions, each time a different emotion. With Betty June in my bedroom I learned *mirth;* with myself in the Argonne I learned *fear;* with my father in the basement of our house I learned

> *frustration*; with Jane Mack in her summer cottage I learned *surprise*; with my heart, in my hotel room on the night before this last day, I learned *despair*, utter despair, a despair beyond wailing. (220)

The fact that Todd can number the occasions on which he has felt emotion is itself comic, and the five emotions he does feel are, at best, curious. He doesn't mention love, pity, or compassion, he doesn't mention any of the emotions that involve other people as human beings. What his emotional experiences reveal is his lack of emotion.

Todd's final emotion, despair, ostensibly deriving from his awareness of his imminent death, results in his decision to commit suicide. But it is possible that even here Todd is deluding himself. Todd may have another, less apparent motive for suicide, a motive for which Barth has left numerous clues. On the night before June 21 or 22 Jane innocently comments on Todd's clubbed fingers, and her comment fills him with despair because it reminds him of his heart. He is subsequently unable to have intercourse with her. But it is not the first time Todd has failed in bed. He confesses that in 1936 every fourth attempt at intercourse failed, and by 1937 every other attempt was a failure (156). Late in the book Todd also admits that he's slept with no women since 1937, seventeen years ago. When he sees Marvin Rose for a physical examination, he makes Marvin promise not to tell him the results until the following day, when he plans to be dead. Todd then declines to have a blood test, and at the end of the exam Marvin pats him on the shoulder and says, "I don't blame you. . . . I'd be ashamed, too" (136). Further, Todd lives in an old people's hotel, and two of his best friends are old men. At one point in the book Harrison Mack asks Todd, "You getting senile?" On the very next page Todd forgets three things (143). When Todd fails to have sex with Jane, he, himself, remarks, "Maybe I'm getting senile" (192). Subacute bacteriological endocarditis with a complication toward myocardial infarction, coupled with an ailing prostate, clubbed fingers, and premature senility, are symptoms of venereal disease; a blood test is the only effective method of diagnosis. While all of these details may be merely coincidental, they also may be Barth's last satiric jab at his *alazon* narrator, his last indication that Todd is not the witty *eiron* he would like to be. Instead, Todd is a lonely, diseased old man, fantasizing about his youth.[9]

Thus Barth combines two archetypal comic characters in his creation of Todd Andrews, forcing two contradictory possibilities on the reader. Like the typical *eiron*, Todd is a witty self-deprecator and artist, arranging the plot of his own life and laughing at the pretension and folly of his humorous society. His ancestors in this comic tradition are characters like Aristophanes' Dicaeopolis, Shakespeare's Prospero, Austen's Knightley, and James's Felix Young. Like the typical *alazon*, Todd is a boastful impostor and blocking figure, deluding himself and refusing festivity. Todd's ancestors in this role are characters like Caliban, Emma, and Mr. Wentworth. In *The Floating Opera* Barth achieves a delicate balance of the conflicting possibilities. To avoid the fate of the "town's idle intelligences" the reader must perceive both contradictory possibilities simultaneously. Like Dickens's Pip, Joyce's Bloom, and James's Strether, Todd Andrews exhibits what Dale Underwood deems the essential ambivalence of the great comic hero.[10]

Barth's comedy simultaneously laughs with and at Todd Andrews. To some extent this balance is demanded by the strategy of making the hero the author of his own novel. The reader approaches the novel assuming two comic conventions: first, that the comic artist must remain detached from his characters, viewing them as social and psychological types, manipulating and exposing their human limitations and foibles; and second, that the characters in comedy are most comic when they are detached from each other, standing egotistically aloof from society. Comedy is the social art, and when a character is isolated from the community he is usually a figure of satire. Todd Andrews finds himself in the awkward position of having to fill both of these expectations simultaneously. As the author of the comic *Floating Opera* he must remain detached, laughing at the foolishness of his characters. But as a character in the novel he cannot remain detached without becoming humorous himself. For example, as author he can laugh at the adolescent fumbling of Todd and Betty June reflected in the mirror, and the reader can laugh with him. But as participant in the action, one of the mirrored couple, he cannot laugh without his laughter sounding hollow, even inhuman. Barth balances the two attitudes perfectly, confronting the reader with irresolvable contradictions. In a sense, the comedy is ultimately directed against the reader, against his desire to know which role Todd is playing. In a novel where the possibility of ever knowing anything is obviously a joke, the reader finds himself the butt of that joke.

This is not a particularly enviable position, and it is not surprising that most critics seem uncomfortable with Todd, emphasizing his perverseness and unreliability and concluding that the novel is nihilistic. Barth goes even further in his joke on the reader. Todd Andrews is clearly meant to be a reflection of the reader himself. Born in 1900, the birth of the century, Todd is the representative twentieth-century man. His heart problem is symbolic of the twentieth-century obsession with death, with the possibility that the touch of a button could destroy the whole world as effectively as Todd could blow up the "Floating Opera." From the first, Todd identifies himself with the reader. Early in the novel he advises the reader, "Don't fear for your weak heart; I've one myself" (2). Later he insists, "My answers were your answers" (139).

The novel is thus, in part, a satire on twentieth-century man, on the reader. Barth dwarfs Todd by showing him as a sick, loveless, deluded old man, a boastful impostor, a comic *alazon* pretending to be something he isn't. But at the same time Barth seems to affirm Todd's dissatisfaction with the existence imposed on him and also his potential to create a world, to fictionalize his experience. As *eiron*, Todd insists, "There's little need for weakness, reader: you are freer, perhaps, than you'd be comfortable knowing" (98). This may be the central point of the novel. Barth criticizes the facts of Todd's world (our twentieth-century world), but he celebrates Todd's effort to recreate it. Todd's novel, *The Floating Opera*, may be his last mask, but Barth refuses to strip this one away. The mask works, its comedy enabling Todd to cope with irrationality and absurdity, to survive.

The theme of creating a fictional world around the self is an old one, evident in comic literature from Aristophanes' *The Acharnians*, in which Dicaeopolis comically creates a society of peace around himself, to Shakespeare's *The Tempest*, in which Prospero uses his magic art to create a beautiful island. Todd's effort to rewrite his life may not be as beautiful as Dicaeopolis' or Prospero's, but it is as effective in preserving his existence. In *Labyrinths*, Jorge Luis Borges remarks, "We . . . have dreamt the world. . . . But in its architecture we have allowed tenuous and eternal crevices of unreason which tell us it is false."[11] Todd has dreamt his world, and Barth has left tenuous crevices of unreason that tell us it is false.

In Chapter 6 Todd describes a scene that could be read as a metaphor for the theme of the novel. Praising Cambridge, he observes:

> What makes High Street lovely are the trees and the street itself. The trees are enormous: oaks and cottonwood poplars that rustle loftily above you like pennants atop mighty masts; that when leaved transform the shabbiest houses into mansions; that corrugate the concrete of the wide sidewalks with the idle flexing of their roots. An avenue of edge-laid yellow bricks is the only pavement worthy of such trees, and like them, it dignifies the things around it. Automobiles whisper over this brick like quiet yachts; men walking on the outsized sidewalk under the outsized poplars are dwarfed into dignity. (52–53)

The discrepancy between the outsized trees and the undersized people, between what Todd would like to be and what he is, between the vastness of the universe and his puny efforts to understand it, is comic. Dwarfed by this discrepancy, Todd retains a measure of dignity in his ability to laugh at the discrepancy and to imagine other possibilities. Barth dwarfs Todd by criticizing his delusions; he dignifies Todd by celebrating his creative possibility. The ridicule and the celebration are comically balanced.

The two endings to the novel are both appropriate to the comic form, reinforcing its comic affirmation. From the outset we know that Todd is not going to commit suicide, and the comic question, answered differently in the different endings, becomes "why not?" After his suicide attempt is interrupted by a *deus ex machina* in the 1956 "happy" ending, Todd feels a sudden irrational emotion for the sick Jeanine Mack and excitedly affirms relative values. "There *are* relative values! These, at least, we have, and if they are all we have, then *in no way whatsoever* are they inferior" (271). He returns home and saves Mr. Haecker.

The 1967 ending seems less happy. Now Todd plans not only to kill himself but to blow up the whole "Floating Opera," but he fails as effectively as before. After his suicide attempt is interrupted, he considers trying again but concludes "why bother?" (242). He feels no emotion for Jeanine, and his enthusiasm pales noticeably. "I considered too whether, in the real absence of absolutes, values less than absolute mightn't be regarded as in no way inferior and even lived by. But that's another inquiry, and another story" (246–47). He saves Mr. Haecker as before but notes Mr. Haecker's subsequent and successful suicide.

Most critics prefer the 1967 ending, arguing that its implied nihilism is more credible than the contrived affirmation of the 1956 ending. But the 1967 ending is itself more affirmatively comic than may at first be apparent. The Macks still celebrate their union, and Todd still decides not to commit suicide and affirms the possibility, at least, of relative values. In conventional comedy the hero is usually integrated into society at the end of the action, celebrating the continuity of life either by marriage or by some other device. Todd cannot marry, since he has been the blocking figure in the Macks' union and must be expelled from it, but he does celebrate continuity. He wins the Mack law case, securing three million dollars for Harrison and earning his law firm fifty thousand dollars. He also devotes himself to a new and even more interminable *Inquiry. The Floating Opera* is but an offshoot of Todd's inquiry into his father's death, which is but a chapter in his inquiry into the nature of the "imperfect communication" between father and son. At the end, *The Floating Opera*, the inquiry into Todd's father's death, and the inquiry into his "imperfect communication" are but a small part of the even larger *Letter to my Father.* The quadrupling of inquiries is itself comic, representing a good metaphor for the continuity of life, which is usually symbolized by marriage. So that Todd will not have to pursue his inquiry alone, he invents a reader with whom to share it.

The Floating Opera is, then, a more affirmative novel than has been generally recognized. Todd Andrews displays the ambivalence characteristic of the comic hero, and the plot moves toward both integration and exposure. Like the typical *alazon*, Todd is dwarfed by the discrepancy between his claims and his capabilities. But like the typical *eiron*, he refuses to remain minified, insisting instead on creating his own fictional world. The reader, participating in the comedy by sharing Todd's self-deceptions, shares his triumphs as well. Like Todd, the reader is dwarfed into dignity.

Todd Andrews, then, is a sophisticated artist-hero who comically manages to rewrite his own history and the history of his country, absurdly affirming life over death. Remaining emotionally uninvolved, Todd survives, ironically exposing both his humorous society and himself. Like Todd Andrews, Skipper, in John Hawkes's *Second Skin*, is faced with an absurd world that he must either transform or escape. But in some ways Skipper's problem is more difficult than Todd's. Whereas Todd can survive by relying on an aggressive intellect and a detached ironic wit, which enable him to avoid much human suffering, Skipper can rely only on his bumbling pacifism and on his humorous naiveté and trust, which make him vulnerable to perpetual pain. If Todd is the comic spirit, laughing at himself and his society, Skipper is the comic buffoon, the cause of malicious laughter in others. Yet Barth and Hawkes share the same complex comic balance of attitudes toward their narrators. Todd seems intelligent and witty, but his intelligence masks an ignorance of the heart. Skipper seems foolish and humorous, but his ignorance masks a wisdom of the heart. Both Todd and Skipper ultimately manage, in their own unique ways, to transform their worlds through art. Simultaneously celebrating and ridiculing their protagonists, Barth and Hawkes affirm the power of comedy to ensure survival and continuity.

III.

The Rarer Action
John Hawkes's Second Skin

It is sometimes dangerous to trust an author's comments on his own work, but it is sometimes equally dangerous not to trust him. Schooled in the "intentional fallacy" and wary of authorial pronouncements, modern readers are reluctant to accept uncritically even comments that are accurate and illuminating. Such is the case with John Hawkes. In interviews and essays Hawkes insists that critics have overemphasized the terror and violence of his novels, while underemphasizing their comic form and vision. Thus one of his basic concerns in *Second Skin* was to clarify the general comic intentions in his writing.

> I'm grateful to you for viewing my fiction as comic. . . . I think you're right that reviewers in general have concentrated on the grotesque and nightmarish qualities of my work, have made me out to be a somber writer dealing only with pain, perversion, and despair. Comedy puts all this into a very different perspective, I think. . . . In *Second Skin* I tried consciously to write a novel that couldn't be mistaken for anything but a comic novel. I wanted to expose clearly what I thought was central to my fictional efforts but had been generally overlooked.[1]

Hawkes goes on to define his comic method. "I think that the comic method functions in several ways; on the one hand it serves to create sympathy, compassion, and on the other it's a means for judging human failings as severely as possible."[2] Ignoring Hawkes and the comic form of his novel, critics have emphasized either Hawkes's sympathy and compassion or his severe judgment of human failings, without adequately describing the complex comic balance of attitudes.

The critical disagreement focuses on Skipper, the protagonist and author of *Second Skin.* While Albert J. Guerard insists that the novel is Hawkes's "warmest and most genial" book, "a vision of the will to survive death and abomination and of the power to move from impotence to fertility,"[3] and Susan Sontag observes that the novel is "ebullient and joyous," "about horror surmounted by lushness and love,"[4] critics like Thomas LeClair,

John Kuehl, and Peter Brooks disagree. LeClair argues that Skipper is a "villain." "In his quest for a land where self and environment correspond, where love and freedom are synonymous, he selfishly destroys others. This new Adam . . . is a killer. That he does not mean to kill is no defense."[5] Similarly, John Kuehl insists that Skipper is full of "sterility and death. At the end of the novel's action and the height of its irony, Skipper feels triumphant over death, but we know better."[6] Peter Brooks describes Skipper as a "fat, sweating paradigm of incompetence" whose love is "undiscriminating, misdirected, and repellent."[7] Even critics who note the comedy tend to emphasize either the violence and terror or Skipper's inadequacies, failing to perceive the comic balance between sympathy and antipathy.[8]

The reader's reluctance to accept an author's interpretation of his own work extends to Skipper as well as to Hawkes. As author of *Second Skin*, Skipper's statements are as potentially unreliable, and if critics have ignored Hawkes's conclusions about his novel, they have actively disbelieved Skipper's conclusions about himself. Grasping the fashionable critical handle of "unreliable narrator," critics like LeClair and Kuehl argue that Skipper is a villain, lying to himself and to the reader. In some cases, certainly, Skipper is unreliable. One of the major functions of comedy, as Hawkes notes, is ironic exposure of character and society. But Skipper is often reliable as well. The most difficult task in writing comedy is maintaining the necessary ambivalence of attitude. Reflecting this ambivalence, which is according to Dale Underwood the essence of the comic hero, Skipper is both comic and heroic.[9] He is comic in his self-exposure —his innocence, his limited perceptual and analytic powers, his unconscious contributions to his own problems; he is heroic in his exposure of his humorous society and in his reflection of the comic values—life, peace, integration, grace, and love. An appreciation of the comedy of the book, and particularly of Skipper's role as comic hero, is necessary to a valid interpretation.

From the outset, Skipper takes his place in a recognizable comic tradition. He is the comic innocent, the fool or buffoon who seems constitutionally immune to knowledge. The characters from comic literature who Skipper most closely resembles are the child-victims of Dickens, James, or Joyce. Like Dickens's young Pip, James's Maisie, and Joyce's young Stephen, Skipper is the radical innocent who suffers at the hands of a crass, humorous society that preys on such innocence. Wearing his Good Conduct Medal over his heart and viewing the world through a child's eyes, the comically rotund Skipper is continually baffled by a world full of sharp, hard things that wound his "especially sensitive skin."[10] His response to his world is that of a child. After being brutally attacked by a barrage of snowballs, for example, Skipper pleads with Miranda, "No snowballs" (93); before his nightmarish experience abroad the *Peter Poor* Skipper warns Jomo, "No pushing" (179). Childlike defenses, however, don't work in a world where even mayonnaise stains are "mysterious" (29).

Children's innocent perceptions and responses to the adult world are comic in themselves, as Dickens, James, and Joyce knew, but in Skipper's case the comedy is intensified by the incongruity between his childish responses and his two-hundred-pound frame, his naval background, and his age. Skipper is too old, and as a navy man should be too experienced, to have retained such innocence. For instance, one would expect a fifty-nine-year-old retired naval officer and father to have had some experience with sex, and yet when Skipper sees Miranda's enormous black brassiere dangling from a hook in the hold of the *Peter Poor*, he is perplexed. " 'Jomo,' I said, 'what's that?' " (183). As in Dickens's novels, the inanimate world in *Second Skin* takes on malevolent life as the brassiere becomes an "albatross" for Skipper, and Miranda's bosom becomes an "unleashed animal" (52).

Throughout the novel, the world's impingement on Skipper is imaged in sexual terms, with the usual roles reversed. Early in the book, for example, Skipper's daughter, Cassandra, insists that Skipper have himself tattooed with the name of her dead husband, Fernandez. Skipper associates the tattooing with an earlier homosexual attack by the mutineer Tremlow. Thus, symbolically, Cassandra sexually violates Skipper by insisting that he submit to the tattooing. Because he loves his daughter so deeply, Skipper willingly submits. Later in the book the sexual roles are again comically reversed, this time with Skipper and Miranda. After the high-school dance Miranda seduces Skipper in order to divert him from his efforts to protect Cassandra. She lures him out into her broken car, wraps her scarf around his neck, and thrusts her naked buttocks into his lap. As with Jane Mack and Todd Andrews in *The Floating Opera*, the usual roles of seducer and seduced are inverted as Skipper "escapes" from Miranda and rushes into the safety of the house.

Like the children in this comic tradition, Skipper is exposed to one violent attack after another. Indeed, the piling up of violence itself reflects the exaggeration typical of comedy. As John Graham notes, "*Second Skin*, reduced to 'plot,' could seem a series of demonic pratfalls played by Charlie Chaplin or Peter Sellers."[11] Throughout the novel various knives, lizards, snakes, needles, and missiles lacerate, puncture, smash, rip, and otherwise violate Skipper's sensitive skin. Yet, like the fool or clown of traditional comedy, Skipper is resilient, always seeming to emerge essentially unharmed. His recoveries fill him with pride, for he is a willing victim, a parodic Christ figure, who is happy to "neutralize" the world's "poison" with his own suffering (5). Indeed, Skipper consistently gives the impression that he wouldn't be completely happy if he weren't allowed to suffer "heroically." While this attitude elicits admiration from the reader, it elicits ridicule as well. Speculating on the future of comedy, Walter Kerr asks, "What if despair itself is the new heroic posture, the new pretense to greatness? What if there is, after all, an aspiration open to ridicule: contemporary man's aspiration to be known as the most wretched of all beings?"[12] By having Skipper dwell on his numerous affronts with such curious pleasure, Hawkes may be satirizing the modern pose of despair and anguish. Sympathy and ridicule are thus carefully balanced in Skipper's affirmation of his suffering.

Because Skipper closely resembles the child-victims of earlier comedy, the discrepancy between his innocence and his age is doubly comic. Further, Skipper's innocence repeatedly results in his humorous misinterpretation of serious events. In his effort to neutralize the world's poison with his own suffering, Skipper often invents absurd enemies while remaining ignorant of real evil. In six structurally parallel scenes, Skipper's comic misinterpretation exposes the dangers of his innocence. Early in the book he describes a journey he took with his daughter and her child in a bus full of sailors. When a tire blows out and the bus skids off the road, Skipper begins to manufacture enemies. "I thought of the two of us alone with a hundred and one sailors cut down and left for dead by a pack of roving and mindless Mexicans" (36). Anxious to protect Cassandra against evil, Skipper harbors this fantasy until he finally perceives that the bus has crashed not on the edge of a stronghold of Mexican bandidos, but on the edge of an army camp. While three AWOL soldiers proceed to "kiss" Cassandra, Skipper feels curiously relieved because "whatever I had to guard Cassandra against it was not the Mexicans" (38).

The second scene follows the same pattern, with Skipper fearing his fantasy while remaining oblivious of real evil. Lured out of the high-school dance by a little girl obviously employed by Miranda, Skipper encounters a barrage of ice balls and, in his innocence, absurdly misinterprets.

> But I stopped. Listened. Because the air seemed to be filled with low-flying invisible birds. Large or small I could not tell, but fast, fast and out of their senses, skimming past me from every direction on terrified steel wings and silent except for the unaccountable sharp noise of the flight itself. One dove into the snow at my feet—nothing but a sudden hole in the snow—and I stepped back from it, raised my hands against the unpredictable approach, the irregular sound of motion, the blind but somehow deliberate line of attack. Escaped homing pigeons? A covey of tiny ducks driven berserk in the cold? Eaglets? (86)

Eventually Skipper figures out that the "birds" are actually snowballs, and again he is curiously "relieved." As he flails about in the snow, bleeding, snowballs hitting him "full in the face—my relief was complete and I knew that this time at least I had nothing to fear from any unnatural vengefulness of wild birds" (87). Next time, of course, he may have to fear vengeful wild birds, but not this time. He is not yet finished misinterpreting this scene, though. Having discerned that he is under a snowball attack, he tries to pinpoint the assailants. His first thought is of Tremlow. "Tremlow! Come out and fight!" (88), he cries, absurdly, since he hasn't seen the mutineer in years. His second thought is of island lovers. "Could this be the activity of island lovers? nothing better to do?" (87). Finally Skipper reluctantly concludes that Jomo might be responsible.

The next two parallel scenes of misinterpretation involve Miranda. After the dance, as Miranda tries to seduce Skipper in order to prevent him from protecting Cassandra, he misinterprets again. "Drunk? Out of her mind with passion? Or spiteful? Who could tell?" (96). Of course the reader can tell, if Skipper can't, and even Skipper vaguely "perceived a cruel motive somewhere" (96). Later Miranda accompanies Skipper in a frantic car chase on the beach. Skipper thinks Cassandra and Jomo are in the car, and he hopes to "save" Cassandra by catching it. But Miranda knows that only Bub is in the car, decoying Skipper.

She throws her arms around Skipper and does her best to make driving difficult. "Her hair flew into my eyes and even into my open mouth. And tongue, teeth, hair, I was trying to breathe through my nose and gagging, choking, but somehow keeping my grip on the wheel and driving on. But was she trying to comfort me, encourage me, even love me, at least urge me to great daring after all? Had I been wrong about Miranda?" (192).

Two final scenes complete the series of parallel misunderstandings. On board his boat, the USS *Starfish*, before the mutiny, Skipper looks out of his porthole at sunrise and sees a lifeboat being lowered down the side. Again his explanation is outrageous: "squall? tidal wave? another ship between ourselves and the sun?" (136). With a mutiny obviously brewing all around him, his greatest worry is that he will be seasick, and he concludes with relief, "I knew I wasn't going to be sick this time, had nothing to fear from my ocean nausea now" (142). Later in the novel, abroad the *Peter Poor*, Skipper innocently misinterprets evil a final time. When Bub hits him on the head with a tire iron Skipper wonders, "Mishap with the boom? Victim of a falling block? One of the running lights shaken loose or a length of chain?" (184).

The pattern is the same in nearly every case. Faced with real evil and an obvious tangible source of suffering, Skipper imagines other and absurd possibilities, feeling relief when those fears prove illusory. The repetitive doubling of scenes intensifies Skipper's comic exposure.

Skipper's innocent misinterpretation of events results in a kind of paralysis or inaction on his part. While claiming to be courageous, he evidences what appears to be inertia at crucial moments when action might seem advisable. Two scenes in particular illustrate Skipper's comic inaction—the bus wreck and the mutiny. In both cases Skipper thinks about conventional heroism but remains unconventionally passive while the violence coalesces around him. After the "nightmare accident," worried about Tremlow and Mexicans, Skipper thinks of himself as "awake, alert, ready for anything. . . . I became the solitary sentry with quick eyes for every shadow" (38). With a hundred sailors on hand to protect them, Skipper takes Cassandra in a "roller skating stance" and skates away from the bus out into the desert. When the three AWOL soldiers appear on the horizon, moving almost in slow motion, Skipper seems paralyzed. He awakens Cassandra, and together they listen as the soldiers crawl up to the fence. When the three heads finally appear, they move comically, mechanically, in unison.

> And as Cassandra and I knelt side by side in the sand, stiff and exposed and red-eyed in our animal positions, together and quiet but vulnerable, the three heads began to move in unison, turned slowly, imperceptibly, to the right and then to the left, in unison scanning the horizon and measuring the potential of the scene before them. The tops of the heavy helmets and the tips of the chin cups reflected the moon; in the sharp little faces the eyes were white. Soldiers. Raiders. Pleased with the scene. (39)

Hypnotized by these "pop-ups in a shooting gallery" (39), Skipper stands by, urging Cassandra to "be brave," while the soldiers take their turns "kissing" her, one of them even drooling "foam, foam, foam!" down the front of her frock. The scene is doubly comic because of Cassandra's willing participation. While Skipper stands inert, worrying about Cassandra's innocence, his "teen-age bomb" asks for more. "Give me your gun, please," she begs of the last soldier. "Please show me how to work your gun" (43).

The same comedy of inaction is evident in the Tremlow mutiny scene. Throughout the day of the mutiny, Skipper does his best to ignore the fact that anything unusual is happening. After wondering whether the lifeboat being lowered outside his window is a squall or a tidal wave, Skipper watches Tremlow working in the lifeboat. "Started painting the shack yet, Tremlow? How about knocking off early for a little boxing? . . . By the way, Tremlow, . . . who told you to take the tarp off the lifeboat? The tarp's supposed to be on the lifeboat at all times. See to it, will you?" (137–38). Skipper is curiously proud of his ability to evade knowledge of evil. "But at least I had been too quick for Tremlow, once again had managed to avoid his deliberate signs of insubordination" (138).

While Skipper assists Mac, the chaplain, with mass, he notices Sonny trying to push his way to the front of the communion line. Obviously Sonny wants to warn Skipper about the mutiny, but Skipper only smiles, thinking he's just anxious to get his wine and wafer. While Skipper wipes off Sonny's mouth, Sonny tries to explain the situation: "I think they means to kill all the officers and dump the bodies in the lifeboats!" Skipper admits that Sonny was "never wrong, . . . so I spent the day in my damp bunk reading" the Bible (141). The causal *so* pinpoints the comedy. Precisely because a mutiny is under way, Skipper retires to his cabin to read.

When the violence finally commences, Skipper is humorously inactive. While Tremlow pummels Skipper, brushing aside his feeble defenses, Skipper thinks "it wasn't fair," and he reasons with Tremlow between blows. "Wait a minute . . . you'll be sorry. . . . You're on duty" (146). Even when the whole disloyal crew piles on, Skipper remains baffled. "There seemed to be a purpose in that struggle, but still it escaped me" (146–47).

Although Skipper's innocence, his misinterpretation of events, and his inaction seem comically discrepant with his avowed heroism, his childlike response assures a measure of reader indulgence and sympathy. But innocence is often dangerously close to ignorance, a fact that Henry James and Jane Austen exploited in their comedies of manners, and Skipper's ignorance of evil seems itself sometimes evil. When Emma Woodhouse and Isabel Archer, for example, wield their naiveté and innocence like a sword, Austen and James comically expose them. Similarly, when Skipper's aggressive innocence makes him an "accomplice" to the evil forces around him, Hawkes exploits the comedy. According to Hawkes, while comedy serves "to create sympathy, compassion," it's also a means "for judging human failings as severely as possible; it's a way of exposing evil (one of the pure words I mean to preserve) and of persuading the reader that even he may not be exempt from evil."[13] Like the other characters in this comic tradition, Skipper is not exempt from evil, and Hawkes exposes his pretensions to exemption.

Skipper seems most culpable in his ludicrous attempts to protect his daughter against the loss of an innocence she never had. Wearing his good conduct medal and his shore patrol armband, Skipper thinks of himself as Cassandra's "guardian, her only defense" (81). He also thinks of himself as her "boyfriend," her surrogate lover. "I felt her knee, her hip, once more her breasts" (11). In his role as boyfriend, lover, father, and guardian, Skipper closely resembles the blocking figure, the *pharmakos* or "refuser of festivity" of traditional comedy. As I noted earlier, in conventional romantic comedy two lovers are opposed by a blocking figure, usually paternal, who disrupts the lovers' union. Usually, the lovers manage to overcome or convert the blocking figure and celebrate the integration of society through their own marriage.[14] In *Second Skin*, Cassandra and Fernandez (later replaced by Jomo) are the lovers, and Skipper is comically both pander and blocking figure.

Although Cassandra seems to want nothing more throughout the novel than to be left alone with her unsavory paramours, Skipper insists on interfering. Inexplicably, he accompanies Cassandra and Fernandez on their honeymoon. Sitting between them in the car, he "saw her breasts heaving again and knew that everything was up to me" (116). He urges Fernandez to kiss the bride, wishing that he himself could kiss her, and he refers to his daughter as "my little bride at last." Fernandez, drunk and loutish as he is, recognizes the implications of the statement. "My bride, Papa Cue Ball . . . you misunderstand, Papa Cue Ball" (116). While Fernandez flashes "cheesecake" at Cassandra, Skipper bounces Cassandra's "purse" on his lap, finally getting up the courage to open it. "How long now had I been waiting for an excuse to open that purse?" (118). When they arrive at the decaying Honeymoon Hide-Away, the happy triad sits down to a wedding feast. Hawkes is careful to make the feast symbolic of Skipper's and Fernandez's joint participation in the destruction of Cassandra. Fernandez has been calling Cassandra "Chicken" during the car ride, and the main dish in the feast is chicken. Skipper's description of the scene makes him seem cannibalistic. "Oh the tortured chicken skewered and brown and lacerated, running with pink blood and some kind of thick peppered sauce, chicken that fell away from the bone and in the mouth yielded first the delicate flavor of tender white meat and the unexpected pain of its unleashed fire" (123). After finishing off the "chicken," they eat dessert—"candy"—Cassandra's other nickname. The point seems to be that Skipper helps to devour Cassandra through his overprotection of her. As both pander and blocking figure, he is comically culpable for her death.

Skipper's willing victimization and his effort to "protect" Cassandra do seem to blind him to real evil. Emphasizing Skipper's culpability and ignoring Hawkes's comments on the novel, critics have concluded that Skipper is himself evil. But although Hawkes obviously exposes Skipper's unconscious participation in his humorous society, and although Skipper's comments are sometimes misleading or unreliable, Hawkes also celebrates

Skipper's capacity for love and graceful action, and Skipper's account of himself is sometimes both reliable and illuminating.

Hawkes describes a "constant" in comic literature

> from Quevedo, the Spanish picaresque writer, and Thomas Nashe at the beginnings of the English novel, down through Lautréamont, Céline, Nathanael West, Flannery O'Connor, James Purdy, Joseph Heller, myself. This constant is a quality of coldness, detachment, ruthless determination to face up to the enormities of ugliness and potential failure within ourselves and in the world around us, and to bring to this exposure a savage or saving comic spirit and the saving beauties of language. The need is to maintain the truth of the fractured picture; to expose, ridicule, attack, but always to create and to throw into new light our potential for violence and absurdity as well as for graceful action.[15]

Of *Second Skin* in particular Hawkes insists, "The novel is about a bumbler, an absurd man, sometimes reprehensible, sometimes causing the difficulties, the dilemmas, he gets in—but ending with some kind of inner strength that allows him to live. . . . We do have, in effect, a survivor. This is the first time, I think, in my fiction that there is something affirmative."[16] Thus Hawkes thinks of Skipper as an "affirmative" character with a capacity for "inner strength" and "graceful action."

If Skipper is comically exposed and ridiculed, even partly blamed for his own and others' suffering, he is also attractive and loving. For one thing, from the perspective of his wandering island he candidly recognizes his earlier failures. He realizes that he has been "accomplice, father, friend, traveling companion, yes, old chaperon, but lover and destroyer too" (175–76). At one point in the book he even anticipates critical objections to his behavior. "High lights of helplessness? Mere trivial record of collapse? Say, rather, that it is the chronicle of recovery, the history of courage, the dead reckoning of my romance, the act of memory, the dance of shadows" (162). Indeed, from the proper perspective, Skipper's innocence, his misinterpretations, even his inaction, may be viewed as heroic after all. If Skipper is exposed, he also exposes his humorous society and forces the reader to reevaluate his own conventional notions of heroism.

To understand Skipper's unconventional mode of heroism it is necessary to examine briefly his alternatives. No matter how bad Skipper may at times seem, his world is so much worse that by contrast his goodness seems irreproachable. His world (our twentieth-century world condensed and concentrated) is a world governed by Pacific War Time, a world in which deathly landscapes predominate: the destructive ocean, the arid desert, the alien and brutal city, the lifeless black islands of the warped imagination. It is a world in which parents and children commit suicide and wives seduce whole crews of sailors in the U-Drive-Inn. Every time Skipper turns his Christian other cheek, someone or something smashes it in.

The most vivid representative of this wartime society is Miranda. The very antithesis of a great earth mother, Miranda, with her overwhelming mammalian bosom and shocking yellow pants, perpetrates violation after violation. First, she destroys Pixie's baby-bottle nipples and disposes of the milk. Next, she puts Skipper's old uniform on her dressmaker's dummy and symbolically defiles it with catsup. Finally, she presents Skipper with his daughter's fetus, decoratively wrapped in red, white, and blue paper. Enemy of life and sexuality and regeneration, Miranda is symbolic of America's, the world's, death and hatred.

In the context of such a world, Skipper's misinterpretation and inaction becomes, in a curious way, heroic. In *Eyeless in Gaza*, Aldous Huxley clarifies this kind of heroism. With the assumption that "means determine ends," Huxley argues:

> Force may subdue, but Love gains. . . . For love is self-energizing. Produces the means whereby its policy can be carried out. In order to go on loving, one needs patience, courage, endurance. But the process of loving generates these means to its own continuance. Love gains because, for the sake of that which is loved, the lover is patient and brave.
>
> And what is loved? Goodness and the potentialities for goodness in all human beings—even those most busily engaged in refusing to actualize those potentialities for goodness in relation to the lover himself. If sufficiently great, love can cast out the fear even of malevolently active enemies.[17]

This seems an accurate description of the theme of *Second Skin*. If Skipper responded to his enemies with the forthright action demanded by critics and typical of epic heroes, he would be using violent means to overcome violence. But if "means determine ends" the result could only be more violence. What Skipper heroically refuses to do is to use society's methods to combat society. Instead, faced with a world that seems to demand violence, Skipper practices love and forgiveness, relying on his "strength and grace" to pull him through (3). As a self-avowed "man of love" and "man of courage" (1) he "defeats" Miranda, Gertrude, Cassandra, and the others by continuing to love them even when they actively work to subvert his love.

Throughout the book Skipper refuses to use society's methods to defeat society. When Fernandez gives Skipper his razor blade so he can defend himself against an imagined attack by a drunken sailor at the Honeymoon Hide-Away, for example, Skipper throws the weapon away and buys the sailor a beer, preferring to befriend him if possible (129). Similarly, when Skipper is required to wear a gun on shore patrol duty, he transforms it into a T-bone steak (155).

Although Skipper's response to violence thus initially seems comic, in the context of his humorous society it becomes heroic. Skipper's inaction is a refusal to use evil means to overcome evil; his misinterpretation is the first step in envisioning a new and more hopeful world. His creation of the wandering island at the end seems to confirm the validity of his claim to courage.

Skipper is brave in his refusal to be brave in the classic sense of the world. His heroism lies in his ability to recognize love and to celebrate the rhythm of life, the comic rhythm. The episode of Tremlow's mutiny is a good illustration of Skipper's comic heroism. What appears on first analysis to be an inadequate response turns out to be an example of his comic perspective. When Sonny warns Skipper that Tremlow means to kill him, Skipper retires to his cabin and falls asleep with the New Testament over his eyes, guided by the Christian virtues of love, compassion, and forgiveness (142). When Sonny later recounts Tremlow's method of stirring the men to mutiny—dancing the hula-hula in a grass skirt—Skipper perceives the ludicrousness of the whole episode. "It must have been amusing, Sonny," he remarks (144). Finally, Skipper refuses even to let Sonny use violence to prevent the mutiny.

> Sonny began to swing high the axe, but I stayed his arm, for a long moment could only stand there waiting, holding my breath, surveying that ludicrous scene of Tremlow's plan. Because there was Tremlow in the moonlit pilothouse, alone on the bridge, and he was wearing only the long grass skirt and the sweat of the dance was still bright and slick and heavy on his arms, his shoulders, his long muscle-banded back. (145)

As usual, Skipper suffers physically for his adherence to his principles, but he is able to maintain his comic perspective. As Tremlow sails away with the mutinous crew, Skipper knows he could blast him out of the water with the ship's guns, but he prefers to "let him go on dancing," and he reports the men "missing in action" (148).

Through most of the novel Skipper maintains this comic perspective, refusing to adopt society's methods of heroism to gain his ends. But on three occasions he does act like a conventional hero, and the consequences of such "heroism" reveal its inadequacy. The belly bumping contest at the high-school dance is the first instance of Skipper abandoning his courageous passivity and adopting a classically heroic role. On the one hand the contest is a parable of Skipper's survival, of his ability to endure humiliation. The very rhythm of the contest reflects the rhythm of the novel: "Bump and shudder and recover" (90). Throughout the novel objects, people, events collide with Skipper, he shudders, and he recovers. But the contest is also a parody of the classical heroic test of manhood. Pushed into the arena by the crowd, Skipper participates with enthusiasm, uncharacteristically enjoying the competition and violence. The episode is couched in mock-heroic language. It is an "obscene tournament," a "night of trials" in which "the fat began to fly" (89). When Skipper skillfully wins the title of "king of the fat" from old Uncle Billy, he feels triumphant, "as if at last I had struck the high gong of the carnival" (92). But when he looks around he realizes that everyone has gone home, that he is alone, and that Cassandra is in the clutches of Red, Bub, and Jomo. The consequence of his "heroic" victory in the contest is the pregnancy of his daughter, the pregnancy that ultimately results in her suicide.

The second episode in which Skipper adopts a conventional heroic role is the car chase with Bub on the beach. Thinking that he is pursuing Jomo and Cassandra, Skipper finally runs Bub into the sea. When he realizes his mistake, he calculatedly hits the young boy in the face. "I pulled back my arm and made a fist and drove it as hard as I could into Bub's nose. I held him close for a moment and then pushed him away, let him go, left him rolling over in the cold black water where he could fend for himself" (196). Parodying the style of a men's magazine, Hawkes allows Skipper some revenge for the suffering imposed upon him by Bub and the others. But again violent action backfires. While Skipper is punishing Bub, Miranda drives away, and Skipper subsequently arrives at the lighthouse too late to prevent Cassandra's suicide. Having lost his courageous passivity for a moment, Skipper also loses his daughter. Trying to defeat violence by violent means, Skipper is himself defeated.

The final instance of Skipper adopting a heroic pose is his confrontation with the green iguana on his wandering island. Catalina Kate has retired to the swamp to have her baby, and Skipper follows her. When he arrives he discovers that a giant iguana has attached itself to Kate's naked back. Immediately Skipper acts. "Just leave him to me," he swaggers. "So I straddled her—colossus over the reptile, . . . I prepared to grapple with the monster" (106). He thinks of himself as Saint George battling the dragon. Again the episode is described in mock-heroic terms, and again Skipper risks being defeated by his own misguided heroism. But Skipper has learned something from his past experience, and he withdraws before doing any real damage. "Well, Kate. . . . Got us licked, hasn't he. . . . He means to stay right where he is until he changes his mind and crawls off under his own power. So the round goes to the dragon. . . . There's nothing to do but wait. . . . We'll have to be patient" (108).

With the exception of these three occasions (and the third is only half an exception), Skipper practices patience and passivity throughout the novel. Heroically refusing to become evil himself, he celebrates love, forgiveness, and virtue. This is, of couse, not the first time in literature that such action has been celebrated. In *The Tempest*, for example, Prospero responds similarly. With his enemies at his mercy, Prospero renounces vengeance.

> Though with their high wrongs I am struck to th' quick,
> Yet with my nobler reason 'gainst my fury
> Do I take part. The rarer action is
> in virtue than in vengeance.[18]

Filled with "the virtue of life itself," Skipper similarly concludes, "How satisfying that virtue always wins" (98–99). From the point of view of conventional heroism—forthright action, manly strength—Skipper is a comic failure. From Hawkes's point of view, Skipper's "inaction" is "the rarer action," and his misinterpretations are an effort to dream a better world.

The allusion to Prospero is not gratuitous. In a novel full of literary allusions, references to *The Tempest* form an important and meaningful pattern. Critics have noted the allusions in passing, but no one has explained their function in the novel. Stanley Kaufmann goes so far as to suggest that the references "do not cohere and possibly are included only because Hawkes saw no reason *not* to include them."[19] *Second Skin*, however, resembles *The Tempest* in several ways, and the resemblances help to clarify Skipper's role and Hawkes's attitude.

The most insistent echo of *The Tempest* is, of course, Miranda's name. Skipper himself points out the allusion. "For a moment I seem to see both magic island and imaginary girl" (5). But the name is ironic, referring not to Prospero's lovely, innocent daughter, but to Skipper's "old antagonist on a black Atlantic island . . . my monster, my Miranda" (5). Skipper's Miranda is more like Shakespeare's Sycorax. With her "black eyes and sockets, uncombed hair, white face" (201), with her "witches' fire" (63) and her asthma powder that produces "smoke enough to form a genie" (66), with her "maniacal chest" (65), her "wheezing" cough (203), and the "shapeless squid" of yarn that "lived in the cave of [her] sewing bag" (70), Miranda controls her black Atlantic island much as Sycorax did her island before Prospero arrived. At one point in the novel Skipper appropriately thinks of himself as "old Ariel in sneakers" (162), for the widow imprisons him on her island as effectively as Sycorax did her Ariel in *The Tempest.*

Like the widow, Cassandra, with her gray eyes and blonde hair (12) parodies the typical Shakespearean romance heroine. For example, while Shakespeare's Miranda is innocent and naive, Cassandra is sexually athletic and perversely experienced.

If Miranda and Cassandra are parodies of Shakespeare's heroine, Fernandez is a parody of the romantic prince Ferdinand. Cast in the lover's role and echoing the prince's name, Fernandez turns out to be more of a Caliban, as his description suggests. A sleazy, ill-tempered laggard, Fernandez holds up his trousers with "the feathery translucent skin of a rattlesnake" (4) and has "a breath smelling of hot peppers, dark and deeply socketed nostrils, flat smoky brown skull" (4).

Like Fernandez, Tremlow is a kind of Caliban, leading the mutiny against his superior, but he is also curiously reminiscent of Trinculo, the bumptious would-be mutineer in *The Tempest.*

Like Caliban, Tremlow is "a devil, a born devil,"[20] but like Trinculo, he is potentially comic. Dancing the hula in his grass skirt, Tremlow recalls Trinculo comically hiding under Caliban's gabardine.

Although Skipper sees himself as Ariel (the only other "Ariel" on the black Atlantic island being attached to Red's car radio), he is actually more like Gonzalo in his naive effort to imagine a better world. Like Skipper, Gonzalo is radically innocent. Awakening to find Antonio's sword drawn to kill him, for example, Gonzalo accepts the explanation that a "whole herd of lions" was menacing them nearby. "Heaven keep him [Ferdinand] from these beasts," Gonzalo prays, his willingness to believe the unlikely explanation recalling Skipper's absurd fear of vengeful birds and Mexicans.[21] Further, the various characters in *The Tempest* perceive Prospero's island in conflicting ways, and the island actually becomes for each what each imagines it to be. For Antonio it is a desert, while for Gonzalo it is a paradise. "Here is everything advantageous to life," Gonzalo exclaims. "How lush and lusty the grass looks! How green."[22] Like Gonzalo, with nearly everyone else perceiving only death and darkness, Skipper creates an island paradise by imagining it.

The allusions to *The Tempest* serve several purposes. First, standing behind *Second Skin*, *The Tempest* establishes the comic norms on which the novel is based, norms reflected in Prospero's and Skipper's "rarer action." While critics complain that norms are absent from much contemporary fiction, making judgment of action and character difficult, Hawkes supplies norms through allusion. Second, Hawkes remarks, "I think that to write fiction that portrays the nightmarish aspects of the unconscious is simply to say at the outset that the opposite view is equally true and equally valid. . . . The nightmare simply leads one toward—or the nightmare could not exist without an awareness of—purity."[23] Thus the nightmarish characters in *Second Skin* imply the existence and validity of their opposites. Behind the evil widow Miranda stands the good and innocent Miranda; behind the sleazy Fernandez stands the princely Ferdinand; behind the terrifying Tremlow stands the foolish and powerless Trinculo. Skipper himself recognizes the possibilities. "No matter how stark the scene, no matter how black the gale or sinister the violence of Miranda, still the light of my triumph must shine through. And behind the interminable dead clanking of some salt-and-seaweed-encrusted three-ton bell buoy should be heard the soft outdoor lowing of this island's cows" (48). Behind the ugly modern world lies the possibility of Prospero's and Skipper's magic islands.

Although Skipper compares himself to Ariel, and although he resembles Gonzalo in his innocent effort to imagine a better world, he most obviously parallels Prospero. Like Prospero, Skipper is a betrayed man who, fallen victim to his humorous society, voyages to a magical island where he recovers control over his life and environment through the use of his art. Like Prospero's, Skipper's voyage takes him from a bleak, inhuman world to a green and fertile realm of possibility and imagination. Both the play and the novel are structured on this movement between two worlds—one ruled by death, violence, war, brutality, and hate, and the other ruled by its opposites, life, love, peace, grace, courage, and creation. At the outset Skipper pictures himself, Cassandra, Pixie, and Sonny "wrecked together in a Chinatown cafe" (24), and later he is "tossed up spent and half-naked on the invisible shore of our wandering island" (162).

If Skipper shares Prospero's good qualities of love, patience, virtue, and forgiveness, he also shares Prospero's less attractive qualities. If Prospero is a good man, he is also at least partly responsible for his original shipwreck. By ignoring the affairs of state in Milan and by innocently trusting evil men, he had "awak'd an evil nature" in Antonio.[24] Similarly, Skipper's innocence seems to awaken an evil nature in his enemies. Also, Prospero is, at times, as priggish a protector of his daughter's innocence as is Skipper. Before giving Ferdinand and Miranda his blessing, Prospero offers a curious warning:

> If thou dost break her virgin-knot before
> All sanctimonious ceremonies may
> With full and holy rite be minist'red,
> No sweet aspersion shall the heavens let fall
> To make this contract grow; but barren Hate,
> Sour-eyed Disdain, and Discord shall bestrew
> The union of your bed with weeds so loathly
> That you shall hate it both.[25]

Skipper is, of course, as familiar with these seeds of death as is Prospero.

Most important, Skipper shares Prospero's talent as an artist, his ability to transform the seeds of death into the seeds of life. Although Skipper often seems helpless, it is important to remember that from the vantage point of the wandering island he is in complete control of the characters and action of the story. Like Dickens's Pip, Barth's Todd Andrews, Nabokov's Humbert Humbert, and Prospero himself, Skipper retains complete artistic control over the story he's in, shaping the destiny of both himself and others. "I, Skipper, led the way. I knew the way, was the man in charge—the AI—and there was no mistaking me for anything but the leader now, and they were the faithful followers" (166). Like Prospero, Skipper controls both past and future. He correctly predicts the sex and birthday of his child (children are traditional symbols of comic continuity), and he transforms the black Atlantic island of Miranda's imagination into the blue Pacific island of his own.

Indeed, Skipper carefully transforms every detail of his earlier painful experience into a happy, pastoral idyll. Skipper's father's occupation of mortician becomes Skipper's occupation of artificial inseminator. The unnatural green of tattoos, cars, guitars, and rotting settees becomes the natural green of iguanas, pastures, and trees. The sterile triad of Skipper, Cassandra, and Fernandez becomes the fertile triad of Skipper, Catalina Kate, and Sonny. Kate Smith's "terrible mammalian concussion . . . the loud breasty volume of mother America" (21) becomes Catalina Kate's quiet mothering of Skipper's (or Sonny's) child. Darkness, death, and loss of innocence become light, life, and higher innocence. Hawkes insists that "structure—verbal and psychological coherence—is still my largest concern as a writer. Related or corresponding event, recurring image and recurring action, these constitute the essential substance or meaningful density of my writing."[26] Of course, recurrence, repetition, and symmetry, evident in Skipper's metamorphoses of his experience, are the typical structural devices of comedy.

The basic structural difference between *The Tempest* and *Second Skin* is evident in their endings. Whereas Prospero returns from his magic island to participate in the old but renewed society, Skipper remains on his island. Prospero's triumph is his renunciation of magic and his rededication to responsibilities he had previously evaded. This is a risk Skipper refuses to take. Having escaped his humorous society and created a better world around himself, he will not return. Prospero gives up his art because his old society is repentant, suggesting renewed comic possibility. Skipper can't give up his art, for his old society remains unrepentant and deadly.

Even his created world, however, refuses to be completely Edenic. Hawkes observes, "But even in the most paradisial of the worlds I've created, the roses conceal deadly thorns."[27] Skipper is careful to point out that his island contains a snaky wind, thorns, boils, heat, lizards, a swamp, and fleas, golden though they may be. *Second Skin*, like *The Tempest*, is thus not simply a vision of the triumph of good over evil. Evil still exists, though it is no longer in control or at the center. It is significant that the novel ends with the celebration of a birth in a graveyard and with a baby who "look like the fella in the grave" (209). Having spent his life trying to neutralize the seeds of death, Skipper at the end will accept both life and death, will accept the comic rhythm of recurrence.

Skipper thus reflects the ambivalence typical of the comic hero. He is the fool or buffoon, the comic innocent who exposes himself in ways he doesn't realize, unconsciously contributing to his own and others' suffering. But he is also the hero who exposes his humorous society, and, by espousing the comic virtues of love, patience, and forgiveness, creates a new society around himself. The affirmative comic movement of the plot suggests the novel's theme. As Hawkes concludes, "comic distortion tells us that anything is possible and hence expands the limits of our imaginations. Comic vision always suggests futurity, I think, always suggests a certain hope in the limitless energies of life itself."[28]

In *Second Skin*, as in *The Floating Opera*, the author manages to maintain a precise comic balance of affirmation and ridicule toward his narrator. Like Todd Andrews, Skipper reveals both his ignorance and his artistry, ultimately creating his own comic version of reality. In *Lolita*, Humbert Humbert, the narrator-artist, himself tries to maintain at least the appearance of this authorial balance. Pretending to both the intelligent, ironic perspective of Todd Andrews and the emotional wisdom of Skipper, Humbert does create his own alternative reality. But if, like Barth and Hawkes, Nabokov both celebrates and ridicules his narrator, he is ultimately less charitable toward him. If Barth and

Todd are wry ironists, and Hawkes and Skipper are humorists, Nabokov and Humbert are parodists. In some ways, Humbert is a grotesque parody of both the Meredithian comic spirit and the Shakespearean romance hero, and an embodiment of the very lust and ugliness he pretends to abhor. In *Lolita,* it is ultimately Nabokov, and not Humbert Humbert, who gets the last laugh.

IV.

No Harm in Smiling
Vladimir Nabokov's Lolita

On 14 September 1975, *Parade* magazine ran a cover story on a young European model with the caption, "The New Lolita." Twenty years after its first publication by a Parisian erotica house, Vladimir Nabokov's novel has become a permanent fixture in the popular imagination. Nabokov's nymphet heroine is perhaps more widely known than any other character in recent literature, and the reasons for her popularity are not difficult to discern. Initially, interest in *Lolita* derived from its supposedly erotic subject matter, its use of sexual perversion and taboo. Indeed, in the popular mind the name "Lolita" still conjures up forbidden pleasures with sensuously provoking young women. But scholars and critics quickly perceived that the novel was not "pornographic," was instead a masterpiece structured on intricate patterns of literary allusion, whimsical game-playing, and a uniquely lyrical, if eccentric, style.

Criticism of *Lolita* has thus focused on two major problems, the morality of the book and its stylistic difficulty. Recent critics, regarding the novel as a literary puzzle or cryptogram, have provided useful "keys" and annotations, helping to clarify Nabokov's complex artistry.[1] Although the tricks, puns, and allusions have by no means been exhausted, further analysis of this kind seems unproductive. More interesting are the efforts to rescue the book from charges of immorality, efforts that somewhat distort its true focus. During the flurry of controversy surrounding the publication of *Lolita*, several distinguished critics hastened to its defense. In demonstrating the essential morality of the novel, these critics found themselves defending the narrator, Humbert Humbert, more strenuously than they perhaps intended. Underplaying Humbert's obvious perversion and spiritual ugliness, they focused on his lyric artistry and his love for Lolita.

Lionel Trilling's early essay on *Lolita* is perhaps responsible for initiating this view. Trilling begins by acknowledging that Humbert is "indeed anything but attractive," exposing "his lack of all admirable qualities."[2] But Trilling then goes on to suggest that in the course of the novel the reader becomes less and less willing to fault Humbert, because what Nabokov has really written is "a story about love."[3] For Trilling, the novel is finally about "passion love" or "courtly love," a romantic ideal that had, until *Lolita*, seemed exhausted. Nabokov's outrageous subject matter, Trilling argues, enables him to write about romantic love based in taboo, guilt, and idealization of the beloved. Trilling is not dogmatic about this interpretation; in fact, he concludes with the suspicion that Nabokov may have set "an emotional trap for the reader."[4]

Recent critics have been less tentative than Trilling. Andrew Field, for example, claims that "Humbert falls in love with Lolita, not the Dolly Haze who satisfied the obsessive dream of his childhood, but the real one for the violation of whom he murders Quilty—the embodiment of all Humbert's lecherousness. . . . He has honestly faced everything he did and did not do and thereby cleansed himself of his unclean past."[5] Donald Morton, in a recent study, echoes Field, insisting that "at a fundamental level it [*Lolita*] is a serious story of love."[6] G. D. Josipovici concludes that "with the replacing of lust by love . . . [Humbert] becomes a poet in deed as well as name."[7]

All of these critics begin with the obligatory statement that Humbert is horrible and then go on to show that he is "really" a lover and artist underneath. The first proponent of this approach, of course, was not Trilling but "suave John Ray," Nabokov's parody editor. Like Trilling, Field, Morton, and Josipovici, Ray insists that although Humbert is inexcusably vile, he is also an artist who can express great tenderness and compassion for his nymphet: "I have no intention to glorify 'H.H.' No doubt, he is horrible. . . . But how magically his singing violin can conjure up a tendresse, a compassion for Lolita that makes us entranced with the book."[8] It is a tricky business aligning oneself with a critic like John Ray.

Not all critics, of course, have rallied to Humbert's support. Kingsley Amis, one of Nabokov's few detractors, concludes that *Lolita* is "bad as a work of art . . . and morally bad—though certainly not obscene or pornographic."[9] Amis describes Humbert's prose style as "idiosyncratic noise," a "sustained din of pun," and his "love" for Lolita as "a matter of the senses, even of the membranes; his moments of remorse are few, brief, and unconvincing."[10] F. W. Dupee, in one of the most intelligent reviews of *Lolita*, points out that Humbert is "a thorough creep and no pitiable sick man or aspiring sick soul."[11]

Two basic questions, then, confront us in *Lolita*. First, is Humbert Humbert "really" a lover and an artist or a pervert and a fool, or is he some curious combination of opposites? Second, what is the thematic focus of the novel as a whole? Critics who attempt to answer such questions, of course, risk provoking Nabokov's wrath. In his afterword to the novel, Nabokov sarcastically dismisses "Teachers of Literature [who] are apt to think up such problems as 'What is the author's purpose?' or still worse 'What is the guy trying to say?' " Nabokov insists that his only purpose in writing a novel is "to get rid of" it (313). Nevertheless, the risk seems worth taking, since disagreement about Humbert and the novel's theme has resulted in critical confusion.

E. D. Hirsch, in his *Validity in Interpretation*, insists that "an interpreter's preliminary generic conception of a text is constitutive of everything that he subsequently understands, and . . . this remains the case unless and until that generic conception is altered."[12] An inability to define Lolita's "intrinsic genre" has resulted in imperfect interpretation. For example, following the example of John Ray and Humbert himself, some critics have concluded that the novel is a tragedy. Trilling tentatively suggests that *Lolita* might be "tragic,"[13] Howard Nemerov concludes that it is "the funniest tragedy since *Hekuba*,"[14] and Daniel J. Hughes terms it "tragi-comic."[15] F. W. Dupee and Alfred Appel, however, are probably more accurate in their generic descriptions. Dupee suggests that "if Mr. Nabokov's methods are the usual methods of comedy, they are here carried to new extremes";[16] Appel observes that the novel is a parody of "the confessional mode, the literary diary, the Romantic novel that chronicles the effects of a debilitating love, the *Doppelgänger* tale, and, in parts, a Duncan Hines tour of America conducted by a guide with a black imagination, a parodic case study."[17]

While *Lolita* does parody all of these conventional forms, it also reflects the methods of comedy to which Dupee refers. Thus, the best generic description of the novel is, perhaps, a parody of comic form. In parodying the form of both Shakespearean romantic comedy and Meredithian satiric comedy, Nabokov complicates the character of Humbert Humbert and defines the thematic focus of the book. A description of the "parodicomic" intrinsic genre of the novel should help clarify some of the perplexing critical questions.

Nabokov's parody of romantic comedy is most obvious, and critics have generally acknowledged it. As I noted earlier, in typical romantic comedy two lovers are opposed by a blocking figure, usually societal or paternal, who disrupts the lovers' union. Usually, the lovers manage to escape or convert the blocking figure and celebrate the integration of society through their own symbolic marriage. In *Lolita*, Humbert Humbert and Lolita are one such pair of lovers opposed by a humorous society. In some ways, Humbert resembles the typical hero of romance, "an exceptionally handsome male; slow-moving, tall, with soft dark hair and a gloomy but all the more seductive cast of demeanor" (27). Lolita, with the gray eyes and blond hair typical of romance heroines, is his paramour. In the course of the action, the lovers manage to overcome one blocking figure, Charlotte, through her death, and another blocking figure, the reader, by converting him to their cause. Although the humorous society continues to oppose their union, the lovers manage to escape it, at least temporarily, by leaving on a continental tour.

Like a good romantic comedy hero, Humbert Humbert idealizes his love, anxiously protecting her "purity" and defending her "chastity." Early in the novel he vows "with the most fervent force and foresight, to protect the purity" of Lolita (65), and he insists that he is careful of not "impinging on a child's chastity" (57). "Restraint and reverence" is his "motto" (126). In fact, he is so delicate about any reference to sex that he often reverts to French, "avant qu'on se couche" (24), or to a romantically poetic version of English. When Lolita's dress gets stuck in her crotch, for example, he describes "the frock-fold that had stuck in the peach-cleft" (119). When Lolita fails to live up to Humbert's romantic vision of her, he is appalled at her use of four-letter words and refuses to repeat them in print (172, 285).

Humbert's "protection" of Lolita's "chastity" is absurd, however, since it usually takes the form of an attack on her chastity. Humbert characteristically protects Lolita from everyone but himself, though he is the worst threat of all. While his language is always delicate and pure, his actions are ugly, and the discrepancy between his description of his acts and the acts themselves is ludicrously comic. One of the best examples of Humbert's comic protection of his lover is the masturbation scene early in the novel. Alone with Lolita in the living room of the Haze house, Humbert perceives a chance for bliss. Tussling with his nymphet over an Eden-red apple, Humbert manages to use the friction generated by Lolita's legs across his lap to accomplish a private climax. Describing the entire scene as "chaste," Humbert performs "the obscure adjustments" required to bring about an ejaculation (60). In an effort to preserve Lolita's ignorance, he attributes his heavy breathing and moans of ecstasy to a "tooth-ache" and starts to sing snatches of the song "Carmen," eventually turning the whole sordid scene into a sacramental experience: "Carmen, ahmen, ahahamen," he prays and moans (62). Comically exaggerating masturbation into "the longest ecstasy man or monster had ever known" (63), Humbert continues to insist that since Lolita was "safely solipsized" (62), he has not in any way compromised her tender purity. The ludicrous scene undercuts Humbert's claims of idealism and his concern over Lolita's innocence.

Later in the book, of course, the parody of romantic comedy becomes even more pronounced and ugly. All pretense of idealism and love deteriorates when Humbert transforms his paramour into a whore, bribing her with nickels and dimes "under condition she fulfill her basic obligations" (185) or persuading her "for sixty-five cents plus the permission to participate in the school play" to manipulate him under a desk at school (200).

Humbert, then, is an ugly parody of the typical romance hero. His "protection" of Lolita is really just a method of imprisoning her in his lust, and his "love" quickly degenerates into "a quick connection before dinner" (166). The discrepancy between the two Humberts—the romance hero and the ugly pervert—provides the incongruity necessary for comedy.

Similarly, the discrepancy between the two Lolitas in the book is comic. Humbert's romantic vision of her constantly clashes with the gum-chewing, obnoxious little girl she prefers to be. Nabokov often exposes this discrepancy through linguistic incongruity. In the very first paragraph, for example, Humbert's lovely lyrical description of his paramour is undercut by a single vernacular phrase. "Lolita, light of my life, fire of my loins. My sin, my soul. Lo-lee-ta. . . . standing four feet ten in one sock" (11). Later, when Humbert licks a speck out of Lolita's eye, she says "Goody-goody" while "nictating" (45). Lolita's vernacular, juxtaposed with Humbert's sophisticated vocabulary, constantly exposes the distance between the vision and the actuality. Further, Nabokov keeps us constantly aware that the sensuous female form described by Humbert is actually that of a "seventh-grader" (44). When Humbert lavishes "ethereal caresses" on the "gooseberry fuzz" of "my twelve-year-old flame" (47), we cannot help but laugh. Also, although Humbert does not like to admit it, the "intoxicating brown fragrance" that emanates from Lolita's hair is not the romantic perfume of the sea, but the result of her not taking baths. Finally, Lolita refuses to play the romance-heroine role in which Humbert has cast her. While he idealizes her in proper romantic fashion, she bluntly describes him: "You revolting creature. I was a daisy-fresh girl, and look what you've done to me. . . . Oh you, dirty, dirty old man" (143). Naive Humbert can't believe it. "Was she joking?" he asks. Throughout the novel, then, the discrepancy between Humbert's vision of Lolita's charms and her actual childishness is comic.

By the end of the novel it becomes clear that Humbert, like Todd Andrews with Jane Mack and Skipper with Cassandra, is less the hero of romance than he is the traditional blocking figure, the paternal force preventing his daughter from forming any kind of personal relationship. When Humbert does finally allow Lolita to see other males, he comically lurks in the car, looking on protectively. Lolita, however, like the typical romance-comedy heroine, does escape Humbert with her lover, Quilty, "the only man she had ever been crazy about" (274). Although she doesn't marry him, she does marry Richard Schiller. Thus the novel could be viewed as a parodic romantic comedy, told not from the point of view of the lovers, as is usual, but from the point of view of the blocking figure, Humbert Humbert. At the end, as in traditional romantic comedy, the blocking figure is expelled, and the lovers escape his influence.

But *Lolita* is more than a parody of romantic comedy. If that were an adequate description, the novel would be fairly simple and straightforward. It is, however, more complicated because Humbert himself perceives that he is a fool, that he has been his own deceiver. It is Humbert who writes this parody of romantic comedy, consciously exposing himself. The fact that Humbert is the self-conscious author of his own exposure complicates the form.

Aware of his own foolishness, Humbert knows that he is in danger of losing reader sympathy and support. In order to regain that support, Humbert adopts a rather sophisticated narrative strategy, a strategy that has fooled a number of critics.

His strategy is to write a Meredithian comic novel in which he is both an *alazon* (a boastful impostor and fool) and an *eiron* (a witty self-deprecator and artist). By satirically exposing himself as well as his society and by posing as a poet, Humbert hopes to persuade the reader-juror that he is really a good fellow underneath. In his role as artist and comic spirit, he ridicules his former self in hopes that this ridicule will reflect the reformation that is the function of the comic spirit, according to Meredith.

To understand Humbert's strategy more clearly, we might compare his narrative technique with Pip's in *Great Expectations.* Both *Great Expectations* and *Lolita* are narrated by a character looking back on the foolishness of his earlier life. Pip exposes his foolish love for his dream girl, Estella, and Humbert exposes his foolish love for his dream girl, Lolita. Surveying their past experience, both characters have attained a detachment that enables them to see themselves in a comic perspective. In *Great Expectations*, the reader laughs at the young Pip while admiring the older Pip for his ability to criticize his own folly. By adopting a similar narrative strategy, Humbert hopes to persuade the reader that, like Pip, he has gained a mature perspective on his folly and has been reformed through love. If he can convince the reader that he is really two characters, Humbert the wise narrator and Humbert the foolish actor in a comedy, he can perhaps claim the kind of sympathy we give to Pip. By consciously casting himself in the role of *alazon*, boastful impostor and pervert, Humbert hopes to elevate himself to the role of *eiron*, witty self-deprecator and artist.

Like Pip, Humbert starts by giving himself a comic name. As John Ray notes, Humbert's "bizarre cognomen is his own invention" (5). In the course of the novel Humbert distorts his name comically into Humbug, Humbird, Homburg, and Hamburger, among others, suggesting his comic perception of himself. Similarly, his use of pseudonymous place names implies a comic perspective. When he is on his way to kill Quilty, for example, he leaves Insomnia Lodge and drives down Grimm Road to Pavor Manor, the absurdly appropriate names reflecting the comic aspects of the scene. Earlier in the book, names like Conception Park, Lake Climax, and St. Algebra serve a similar function.

But Humbert isn't content merely to expose himself in this droll way. He also mercilessly berates himself throughout the book. He calls himself "pathetic" (64), a "brute" (195), a "humble hunchback abusing myself in the dark" (64). He describes his romantic plans as "horrible, insane, ridiculous and pitiful" (44), "the mechanism of that dream vacuum wherein revolves a deranged mind" (124). Humbert seems prepared to criticize himself more viciously than any reader possibly could. He criticizes not only his actions, but the very style in which he articulates his criticism. After evoking a lyrical picture of Lolita in the first paragraph, he consciously undercuts himself: "You can always count on a murderer for a fancy prose style" (11). Soon thereafter he hopes that the reader "can still stand my style" (12).

All of these comic devices of self-deprecation are evident in Humbert's most masterfully realized comic scene, the "climax" of the book, "*le grand moment*" (125). From the outset Humbert seems to take a comic view of his first night with Lolita in the Enchanted Hunters Hotel. He sets the comic tone with the names he chooses for the hotel personnel:

> "Mr. Potts, do we have any cots left?" Potts, also pink and bald, with white hairs growing out of his ears and other holes, would see what could be done. . . .
>
> "Would there be a spare cot in 49, Mr. Swine?"
>
> "I think it went to the Swoons," said Swine, the initial old clown. (120)

The comic rhymes and alliteration, and the allusions to pigs and swinishness, establish Humbert's comic tone.

When Humbert finally approaches his sleeping beauty, thinking that his "philter had felled her" (127), the scene remains comically mundane and trivial. The noisy toilets seem to conspire against him, he has heartburn, and to top it all, Lolita has cruelly appropriated both pillows, forcing him to sneak one back when she asks for a drink of water. As Humbert leans over the half-awake Lolita, she confuses him with Barbara, the girl with whom she had shared Charlie's manhood at camp. Humbert comically sees himself in the third person as Barbara, adding a further element of farce to the already farcical situation: "Barbara, wearing my pajamas which were much too tight for her, remained poised motionless over the little sleep-talker" (130).

Then, for the biggest joke on himself of all, Humbert turns to the jury and confesses, "it was she who seduced me" (134). "Sensitive gentlewomen of the jury, I was not even her first lover" (137). By laughing at himself, undercutting his own earlier foolishness, Humbert seeks to gain reader sympathy. By making his lust risible, he hopes to neutralize any moral objections that might be raised. Cleverly, he even manages to implicate the reader in his defense. "Imagine me," he pleads. "I shall not exist if you do not imagine me; try to discern the doe in me. . . . Let's even smile a little. After all, there is no harm in smiling" (131). Once we have smiled with him, he has practically won his case.

If Humbert marshals reader sympathy by exposing his own foolishness, he increases that sympathy by showing how much worse is his humorous society. Although Nabokov claims that he himself has "neither the intent nor the temperament of a moral or social satirist,"[18] his character Humbert has a keen satirical eye for American manners and morals. In the course of the novel he satirizes American songs, ads, movies, magazines, products, tourist attractions, small towns, camps, schools, hotels, and motels, among other things. By satirically exposing the society around him, Humbert, like Todd Andrews, reveals his perceptive wit, thus effectively qualifying his own absurdity.

Humbert's first satiric target is Charlotte Haze, the representative middle-class American clubwoman and moralist. From the first, Charlotte is a neurotic woman who rarely deviates into sense and never fails to miss her own comicality. As Humbert notes, she is "completely devoid of humor" (39). She seriously believes, for instance, that Lolita's spitefulness originated in babyhood when she purposely threw things out of her crib so that Charlotte would have to pick them up (49). Charlotte has no ideas of her own but relies instead on "the wisdom of her church and book club," the comic juxtaposition of the two organizations suggesting their equal importance in her mind (77–78). Humbert observes that Charlotte "did not notice the falsity of all the everyday conventions and rules of behavior, and foods, and books, and people she doted upon" (86). Humbert, of course, is one of the people she dotes upon, and she manages to remain oblivious of his true feelings toward her for some time. Charlotte's banality and self-deception thus make her a proper victim of Humbert's satiric exposure. We cannot feel too critical of Humbert for duping her, since she practically asks to be duped. F. W. Dupee perhaps best summarizes Charlotte's generic attributes: "With her 'principles' which bulk large but weigh little, her vacuous animation, her habit of asserting herself although she has next to nothing in her to assert, Charlotte is the immoral moralist, the loveless romantic, the laughless comic—whatever it is that spoils the party and dampens the honeymoon all across America."[19]

Like Charlotte, Lolita embodies material for satire. Humbert realizes that his nymphet is partially an extension of her mother, and that, as Mrs. Dolly Schiller, she will slip easily into her mother's role. Lolita's potential vulgarity provokes Humbert to satirically expose its causes, and his prime target is the American educational system. Referring to Lolita's incongruous seduction of him in the Enchanted Hunters Hotel, Humbert insists that "modern co-education, juvenile mores, the campfire racket and so forth had utterly and hopelessly depraved" her (135). Lolita herself perceives the humorous education provided her by Camp Q:

> I was taught to live happily and richly with others and to develop a wholesome personality. Be a cake, in fact. . . . We loved the sings around the fire in the big stone fireplace or under the darned stars, where every girl merged her own spirit of happiness with the voice of the group. . . . I fill my life with worthwhile deeds such as—well, never mind what. My duty is—to be useful. I am a friend to male animals. I obey orders. (116)

Lolita, as well as Humbert, sees through the moralistic camp propaganda and ridicules it, a cynic at age twelve. Ironically, although Humbert criticizes Camp Q, it has prepared Lolita admirably for his victimization.

Humbert, however, saves his most pointed satire for Beardsley School. Headmistress Pratt, one of the more obvious caricatures in the novel, describes Beardsley's educational philosophy in terms so absurd that no undercutting comment from Humbert is required:

> We are not so much concerned, Mr. Humbird, with having our students become bookworms or be able to reel off all the capitals of Europe which nobody knows anyway, or learn by heart the dates of forgotten battles. What we are concerned with is the adjustment of the child to group life. This is why we stress the four D's: Dramatics, Dance, Debating and Dating. . . . To put it briefly, while adopting certain teaching techniques, we are more interested in communication than in composition. That is, with due respect to Shakespeare and others, we want our girls to *communicate* freely with the live world around them

> rather than plunge into musty old books. . . . We think, Dr. Humburg, in organismal and organizational terms. . . . for the modern pre-adolescent child, medieval dates are of less vital value than weekend ones." (179–80)

Although Humbert is disturbed by all the meaningless jargon and cant, "two intelligent ladies" assure him that "the girls did quite a bit of sound reading and that the 'communication' line was more or less ballyhoo aimed at giving old-fashioned Beardsley School a financially remunerative modern touch" (180). In other words, this American school has to pretend to be appallingly bad in order to remain funded.

School, camp, and family life are dedicated to integrating the child into American society, and as Humbert points out, Lolita is ideally suited to consumerism:

> She believed, with a kind of celestial trust, any advertisement or advice that appeared in *Movie Love* or *Screen Land*. . . . If a roadside sign said: VISIT OUR GIFT SHOP–we *had* to visit it, *had* to buy its Indian curios, dolls, copper jewelry, cactus candy. The words "novelties and souvenirs" simply entranced her by their trochaic lilt. If some café sign proclaimed Icecold Drinks, she was automatically stirred, although all drinks everywhere were ice-cold. She it was to whom ads were dedicated: the ideal consumer, the subject and object of every foul poster. (150)

To keep his little concubine in tow, Humbert concludes that all he has to do is reward her with "things." After *le grand moment*, for example, he buys her a veritable catalogue of consumer items: "four books of comics, a box of candy, a box of sanitary pads, two cokes, a manicure set, a travel clock with a luminous dial, a ring with a real topaz, a tennis racket, roller skates with white high shoes, field glasses, a portable radio set, chewing gum, a transparent raincoat, sunglasses, some more garments—swooners, shorts, all kinds of summer frocks" (143-44). The satiric thrust of the catalogue is brutally intensified by its juxtaposition with the announcement of Lolita's mother's death.

A society in which death and tennis rackets carry equal weight and significance obviously has little idea of where it is going or why. This apparent purposelessness of American culture is introduced early, in a journey Humbert makes with an American scientific expedition into arctic Canada. No one, including its organizers, seems to know the purpose of the expedition, and the list of supplies is comically inappropriate: *Reader's Digest,* an ice cream mixer, paper caps for Christmas. As Humbert concludes later, the real purpose of the expedition was "hush-hush," and "that purpose was admirably achieved" (36).

In his role as witty comic spirit, Humbert delights in exposing the absurd aspects of American society. Toward the end of the novel he grows even more blunt in his satiric attacks. When Mrs. Chatfield pompously boasts about her moral standards for her daughter, Phyllis, Humbert matter-of-factly intervenes. " 'Oh yes, of course,' I said quietly. 'I remember Phyllis. Phyllis and Camp Q. Yes, of course. By the way, did she ever tell you how Charlie Holmes debauched there his mother's little charges?' " (292). Immediately thereafter Humbert similarly undercuts Quilty's relative, the dentist Dr. Ivor Quilty. Pretending to be interested in a set of false teeth, Humbert succeeds in learning the playwright's address and in arousing the dentist's professional pride. Before leaving, Humbert turns to Dr. Quilty and remarks, "On second thoughts, I shall have it all done by Dr. Molnar. His price is higher, but he is of course a much better dentist than you" (293).

It is easy to identify with Humbert as a comic hero who criticizes himself while undercutting the pretensions of stuffy ladies and pompous dentists. Like Todd Andrews, in laughing at himself and his society, Humbert reveals his comic perspective. In a world gone wrong, a cheap, tawdry world filled with hot fudge sundaes, comic books, shoddy motels, neon, and cement, we have to value the kind of intelligence and perspicacity Humbert seems to embody.

If Humbert thus boasts a comic perspective, he also boasts a potential artistry, continually insisting that he is more of a poet than a pervert. "The artist in me has been given the upper hand over the gentleman," he confesses (73). Referring to *le grand moment,* Humbert presents his strongest argument for reader sympathy: "If I dwell at some length on the tremors and gropings of that distant night, it is because I insist upon proving that I am not, and never was, and never could have been, a brutal scoundrel. The gentle and dreamy regions through which I crept were the patrimony of poets—*not* crime's prowling ground" (133). As an artist, Humbert is concerned with something much more significant and beautiful than mere sex. "A greater endeavor lures me on: to fix once for all the perilous magic of nymphets" (136). In the course of the novel, he does manage to create an ideal romantic creature out of a rather common little girl. "What I had madly possessed was not she, but my own creation, another, fanciful Lolita—perhaps more real than Lolita; overlapping, encasing her; floating between me and her, and having no will, no consciousness—indeed, no life of her own" (64).

As the artist creating a world around himself, Humbert is squarely in a recognizable comic tradition. From Aristophanes' Dicaeopolis, who creates a world of peace around himself; through Shakespeare's Prospero, who conjures up a magical island; to Barth's Todd Andrews, who recreates his own history; and Hawkes's Skipper, who imagines a pastoral paradise, artistic creation has been a central theme of comic art. If the artist-hero cannot integrate himself into an existent society, he manages to create a new society around himself that is much more beautiful than the existent humorous one. Humbert's artistry has persuaded many critics to affirm him. Page Stegner, for example, concludes that "his actions are affirmative rather than negative; . . . they are attempts to recapture and petrify for eternity a piece of the cherished past."[20] Richard Pearce insists that "with his fertile and daring imagination Humbert Humbert made the ugly Lolita into a nymphet of singular beauty. He destroyed her life but also transformed her imaginatively—giving her far more value than she would have achieved on her own."[21] And Robert Uphaus argues that "his creative sensibility transmutes the dull, sometimes hostile facts of ordinary life into living monuments to his comic spirit."[22]

The ending of Humbert's novel seems to reinforce this comic affirmation, reflecting elements of both an exposure comedy, like *Great Expectations*, and a romance comedy, like those of Shakespeare. In an exposure comedy, the deluded protagonist is usually reformed through ridicule. In *Great Expectations*, for example, Pip escapes his dark self, Orlick, overcomes his egotism, and experiences a deep love for Estella, though she marries Bentley Drummle. Humbert's novel ends similarly, as he defeats his bad self, Quilty, criticizes his earlier folly, and confesses real love for Lolita, though she marries her Dick.

Humbert's ending also parallels that of a typical romance comedy. In romance comedy, the lovers escape the paternal blocking figure and celebrate their union. In *Lolita*, the heroine escapes Humbert, marries Richard Schiller, and prepares to live happily ever after with Humbert's money, her unborn child reflecting the promise of social continuity present at the ends of most comedies. The foolish character is converted; the lovers celebrate their union.

The "happy ending" of Humbert's novel has appealed to some critics. F. W. Dupee, for example, concludes that "Lolita . . . has not been destroyed; indeed, she has exhibited the strange capacity of the young to survive the worst abuses."[23] The *Time* reviewer concludes similarly: "From a monstrous relationship a kind of shadow of a good life emerges. . . . Lolita, the perverted child, becomes a true innocent. In the end . . . she is pregnant and happy with a young goon-like husband."[24] Andrew Field insists that the profound moral of Quilty's play has been realized: "That mirage and reality merge in love."[25]

Since the preliminary generic conception of a text determines its interpretation, a reader who, with Humbert, sees *Lolita* as a parody of romance comedy, or as a satiric exposure comedy, will accept Humbert as a comic hero in a tradition comprised of characters like Pip, Emma, Lambert Strether (Humbert notes that a possible pseudonym for himself would have been "Lambert Lambert"), and Skipper. Like them, Humbert seems to possess "essential innocence" (302), obscured by a folly he overcomes.

But Humbert's comic novel is not Nabokov's. In fact, Humbert's self-criticism and artistry is, in some ways, but another and subtler pose, a pose that Nabokov undercuts through parody. If Humbert casts himself in the role of comic hero, Nabokov parodies that role. As I suggested earlier, Humbert's narrative strategy is similar to Pip's in *Great Expectations.* Both characters look back on their prior folly, exposing themselves from their new comic perspective. But the difference between *Lolita* and *Great Expectations* helps to define more accurately Nabokov's method. In *Great Expectations*, the older Pip never fools himself or the reader, and Dickens never criticizes him. Humbert Humbert, however, continually fools both himself and the reader, and Nabokov constantly undercuts him through parody.

In the afterword to *Lolita* Nabokov clarifies his attitude toward Humbert. "My creature Humbert is a foreigner and an anarchist, and there are many things, besides nymphets, in which I disagree with him" (317). In an interview with Herbert Gold, Nabokov is even more explicit. When Gold suggests that "Humbert, while comic, retains a touching and insistent quality—that of the spoiled artist," Nabokov counters, "I would put it differently: Humbert Humbert is a vain and cruel wretch who manages to appear 'touching.' "[26] We needn't, however, go outside the novel to see Nabokov's criticism of Humbert. Throughout the book Nabokov has his character expose himself in ways Humbert doesn't realize.

Humbert's self-criticism, for example, is rather selective. While consciously emphasizing some of his less attractive attributes, he fails to notice others. He never undercuts his boastful vanity, a typical characteristic of the comic *alazon*. Describing himself as a romance hero, he observes, "I was, and still am, . . . an exceptionally handsome male; slow-moving, tall, with soft dark hair and a gloomy but all the more seductive cast of demeanor" (27). By itself this remark does not seem unduly boastful. But repeated dozens of times, it becomes comic. Humbert later describes himself as "a great big handsome hunk of movieland manhood" (41) and boasts of his "clean-cut jaw, muscular hand, deep sonorous voice, broad shoulder" that make him resemble "some crooner or actor chap" (45). He displays "the magic of my manliness" (79) and counts on it to win Lolita back late in the book. "I resolved to make myself especially handsome and smart. . . . bathed and perfumed my delicate body, shaved my face and chest" (270). "Well did I know, alas, that I could obtain at the snap of my fingers any adult female I chose; in fact it had become quite a habit with me of not being too attentive to women lest they come toppling, bloodripe, into my cold lap" (27). After all his insistence on his good looks, he intrudes to reiterate, "I do not know if in these tragic notes I have sufficiently stressed the peculiar 'sending' effect that the writer's good looks—pseudo-celtic, attractively simian, boyishly manly—had on women of every age and environment" (106). Although Humbert thus claims that he is irresistible to women, the action of the novel shows how resistible he really is. His first wife, Valeria, runs off with a taxi driver, and his nymphet, Lolita, runs off with a playwright, having never loved Humbert at all.

Humbert not only boasts about his physical charms, but also insists that he is spiritually and emotionally superior to everyone else. Early in the novel he poses as Christ. "Look at this tangle of thorns," he laments to the reader-juror (11). Later he insists that he is capable of a depth and intensity of bliss unavailable to ordinary human beings.

> I am ready to believe that the sensations I derived from natural fornication were much the same as those known to normal big males consorting with their normal big mates in that routine rhythm which shakes the world. The trouble was that those gentlemen had not, and I *had*, caught glimpses of an incomparably more poignant bliss. The dimmest of my pollutive dreams was a thousand times more dazzling than all the adultery the most virile writer of genius or the most talented impotent might imagine. (20)

Humbert is special. No one, not even a writer of genius, could so much as imagine the heights Humbert has reached. Although he can enjoy normal sexual relationships as well as the next man, his special sensitivities elevate him to an almost religious realm where masturbation must be sanctified with an amen (62). Egotistically isolating himself from the human community, Humbert resembles the comic humors that people the plays of Molière.

Humbert exposes himself unconsciously, but he also consciously lies to the reader, trying to trick him into sympathy. It is important to remember that the purpose of Humbert's novel is self-defense. He imagines that the reader is a jury, sometimes a human jury, sometimes a heavenly court of "winged gentlemen," and that he is arguing for his soul. To save himself, Humbert will use whatever rhetorical strategy seems to work, and his rhetoric shifts to suit his needs. When he wants to show the superiority of his artistic passion, he claims to be a unique individual (20). When he wants to show the generality of his folly, he claims to be merely a poor pervert, one of many sad and harmless similar cases of "innocuous, inadequate, passive, timid strangers who merely ask the community to allow them to pursue their practically harmless, so-called aberrant behavior, their little hot wet private acts of sexual deviation without the police and society cracking down upon them. We are not sex fiends! . . . Emphatically, no killers are we. Poets never kill" (90). Similarly, when it strengthens his case to argue that he is an artist more interested in creation than intercourse, he claims to be a poet (73, 133), but when he wants the reader-juror to believe that he is merely presenting the facts of the case, he underplays his imaginative embroideries on the real situation. "I am no poet," he explains. "I am only a very conscientious recorder" (74).

His other arguments are similarly specious. He claims that his passion is "natural," that he's merely "following nature" (223, 137), and he marshals historical figures from more "enlightened times" to his defense. Humbert argues that Petrarch fell in love with Laureen when she was twelve; actually she was eighteen. He also notes that Dante fell in love with Beatrice when she was eight, neglecting to mention that Dante was only nine at the time and that there was no real romance between them.

If all these bits of contradictory "evidence" don't win his case, Humbert will use the archetypal claim of the rapist, accusing his victim of being the actual victimizer. Humbert blames Lolita's "nymphean evil breathing through every pore of the fey child" (127) for his mistreatment of her. He also speculates on Lolita's being "accused of having impaired the morals of an adult in a respectable inn" (152). Finally, he complains that she took advantage of his weakness all along. "I was weak, I was not wise, my schoolgirl nymphet had me in thrall. With the human element dwindling, the passion, the tenderness, and the torture only increased; and of this she took advantage" (185). According to Humbert, the roles are comically reversed: the twelve-year-old mistreats him while he suffers under her cruelty.

Humbert, however, is a monster all along, from his "slapping Valeria's breasts out of alignment" (89), through his obscene manipulations of Lolita before every breakfast, lunch, and dinner, to his gratuitous murder of Quilty. Yet he continues to claim with a straight face that he is a "tenderhearted, morbidly sensitive, infinitely circumspect hero" (131) with a "credulous, simple, benevolent mind" (202), who is only interested in doing "everything in my power to give my Lolita a really good time" (165). "Imagine me, reader, with my shyness, my distaste for any ostentation, my inherent sense of the *comme il faut*" (249).

Thus, for all of Humbert's self-criticism, he remains unaware of much of his egotism and ignorance. Similarly, his conscious social satire often reflects on him comically. Although he successfully ridicules Charlotte, for example, as a representative middle-class American buffoon, he fails to see that her very inadequacies expose him as well. In some ways Charlotte is very much like Humbert. Charlotte's hopeless passion for Humbert, for example, parallels Humbert's for Lolita. Despite Humbert's ridicule, Charlotte's romantic feelings are not so different from his, belying his claims that his ecstasies are special. Like Humbert, Charlotte writes a "confession," uses French consistently, and deprecates herself as a "shameless little idiot" (70). When Humbert satirizes Charlotte for her foolish passion, he is ridiculing the very quality she shares with him. Later in the novel, frustrated with Lolita, Humbert even more closely and damningly allies himself with his dead wife. He threatens to imprison Lolita in a farmhouse and subject her to Latin lessons "unless her 'present attitude' changed. Charlotte, I began to understand you," says Humbert, adopting Charlotte's methods and vocabulary for dealing with Lolita.

Two more of Humbert's satiric targets, doctors and psychologists, turn back on him as well. "I love to fool doctors," Humbert laughs, as he tricks the Ramsdale doctor into giving him a powerful sleeping potion to use on Lolita (96). On the night of *le grand moment*, however, Humbert discovers to his chagrin that the pills are placebos; it is Humbert who has been duped. Further, like Nabokov, Humbert detests Freudians. He enjoys duping his psychiatrists by inventing dreams and primal scenes to distract them from his real sexual interests, and he is delighted to discover that the doctors have erroneously concluded that he is potentially homosexual and practically impotent (36). But, curiously, after all this ridicule of psychoanalysts, Humbert claims to be one himself. "I am not a criminal psychopath taking indecent liberties with a child. The rapist was Charlie Holmes; I am the therapist" (152).

If Humbert's self-deprecation and social satire often backfire on him, so do his claims of artistry. Like Stephen Dedalus's, Humbert's claims to being a poet far outreach his actual poetic production. In *A Portrait of the Artist*, Stephen's first "poem" is actually a class list:

Roderick Kickham
John Lawton
Anthony MacSwiney
Simon Moonan[27]

Humbert's first "poem" in *Lolita* is also a class list. "A poem, a poem, forsooth!" he cries upon discovering the list of Lolita's classmates (53–54). Humbert's second poem is, like Stephen's villanelle, a pastiche of high and low styles masquerading as a deeply serious work of art. Further, at several points in the novel Humbert unconsciously drops into doggerel that undercuts his pretense of emotion:

> Oh Lolita, you are my girl,
> as Vee was Poe's and Bea Dante's,
> and what little girl
> would not like to whirl
> in a circular skirt and scanties? (109)

Of course, Humbert does write a novel, and while it is not the same novel Nabokov writes, it is rather impressive in its own right.

But although Humbert seems to be shaping his own novel, it is evident that another hand is guiding his. While Humbert seems to have control over character and style, "McFate" (Nabokov) controls the plot. Nabokov's most effective method of exposing Humbert's imposture is the use of extensive comic structural doublings. Two kinds of doubling are typical of comedy. One device is the inclusion of one or more parody characters grouped around the major character to focus his exposure by embodying more clearly his various absurd aspects. In *The Floating Opera*, Barth casts Mr. Haecker in the role of Todd's double. Another comic device is the doubling of scenes in the plot in order to expose their comedy. In *Second Skin*, Hawkes uses this device to ridicule Skipper's absurd misinterpretations in six parallel scenes. Nabokov uses both of these devices to undercut Humbert and his passion.

The sexual affairs that Humbert catalogues early in the novel, for example, function to expose the central situation of Humbert's "love" for Lolita. Humbert traces this emotion to his early love for another nymphet, Annabel Leigh, but Annabel is just the first in a long line of females, young and old, with whom Humbert has had relations. He enumerates the eighty prostitutes and other women in his life, including Monique, Valeria, Marie, Rita, Lolita's school friends, and numerous unnamed twelve-year-olds whom Humbert observes in parks and after school. The repetition and exaggeration of girls, women, lovers, wives, and nymphets renders Humbert's obsession comic. Even after he meets Lolita and confesses his great love for her, he can't resist dreaming about other nymphets who are, in some ways, preferable even to Lolita. The comedy of Humbert's early sex life establishes the context for his later life with Lolita.

Humbert's marriage to Valeria early in the book is the most obvious comic doubling of the central situation, parodically paralleling Humbert's later progress with Lolita. When Humbert marries Valeria she seems like a little girl, and Humbert assumes she is a virgin. But, like Lolita, she ages rapidly, and Humbert soon discovers that he was no more her first lover than he will be Lolita's. Valeria, like Lolita, is an "innocent" who has "mislaid her virginity" (27). Humbert complains, as he will later with Lolita, that "no matter how I stuffed it [her mouth] with love" (28) he can't save the relationship. Like Lolita, Valeria finds the "irresistible" Humbert eminently resistible and leaves him for another man. Her subsequent marriage to Taxovitch is a grotesque parody of Lolita's grotesque marriage to the hard-of-hearing Dick Schiller. Humbert's first impulse upon discovering that the driver of their taxi is Valeria's lover is to shoot them both; later he actually does kill Quilty. Although Humbert is prevented from stomping on Valeria with his boots as he wants to, he is later able to hit Lolita in the mouth (229). Finally, like Lolita, Mrs. Maximovitch dies in childbed. Thus Humbert's marriage to Valeria is a parodic doubling of his later relationship with Lolita, ridiculing the basis of the central situation and exposing Humbert's later protests of true love and compassion.

If Humbert's relationship with Lolita is comically doubled by his relations with other females, Humbert himself is doubled by several caricatures. As I noted earlier, Charlotte Haze is one comic double of Humbert. John Ray, Jr., Nabokov's parody editor, is another. Like Humbert's, John Ray's name is comically doubled: J.R. Jr. Like Humbert, Ray is a professor and pedant who has published "tortuous essays in obscure journals" (18, 7). At one point in the book Humbert is described as "Ray-like" (52). Since Ray is obviously a comic parody, any qualities that Humbert shares with him must be comic as well.

In his introduction, Ray doubles at least two of Humbert's comic claims: that the novel is a tragedy and that it is basically a moral tale. The comic Ray insists that the novel is "a tragic tale tending unswervingly to nothing less than a moral apotheosis" (7). When Humbert comes to similar conclusions later in the text, therefore, we cannot take him seriously. Humbert, too, terms his novel "tragic" (106), and he is, like Ray, a moralist devoted to preserving chastity and purity.

Both Charlotte Haze and John Ray comically double Humbert, but his most significant comic double is Clare Quilty. Most critics have accepted Humbert's treatment of Quilty as a dark alter ego, Humbert's bad self, his psychological *Doppelgänger.* If that is true, then Humbert's killing of Quilty is an heroic act, symbolizing Humbert's triumph over his past, allowing the good artist and lover to shine through. But Humbert misunderstands Quilty's function. Nabokov himself, in his interview with Alfred Appel, ridicules the idea of the *Doppelgänger.* "The bathroom doubled as my study. Here is the *Doppelgänger* theme for you."[28] Quilty is not a psychological double, but a comic caricature who reflects in simplified form the foolishness of the protagonist.

Nabokov emphasizes the comic parallels. Early in the novel, for example, Humbert reads a biography of the playwright and discovers that Quilty wrote *The Little Nymph* and *Fatherly Love* and that "his many plays for children are notable" (33). Like Quilty, Humbert has a little nymph, practices fatherly love of a sort, and makes "many plays for children." The two characters even resemble each other. Both are balding with small, dark mustaches, and both have purple dressing gowns (59, 296). Further, Mary, the nurse at Elphinstone, and Humbert both refer to Quilty as Humbert's "brother" (249, 251).

Quilty comically exposes Humbert by doubling two of his central characteristics, his sexual perversion and his effort to turn his life into comic art. If Humbert manages to blur his perversion, Quilty is obviously a pervert. Like Humbert, Quilty is attracted to little girls, and after freeing Lolita from Humbert he tries to imprison her in his own fantasies. Lolita explains, "He had two girls and two boys, and three or four men, and the idea was for all of us to tangle in the nude while an old woman took movie pictures" (278). Several times in the novel Humbert wishes that he, too, had filmed Lolita (234). At the end, when Humbert accuses Quilty of misusing Lolita, Quilty exclaims, "I saved her from a beastly pervert. . . . I'm not responsible for the rapes of others" (300). Quilty's protest doubles Humbert's own argument to the jury earlier, that Charlie, not he, was responsible for Lolita's loss of innocence (152).

Since Quilty comically reflects Humbert's perversions, it is no wonder that the narrator would like to kill him. But killing Quilty proves more difficult than Humbert had anticipated because, in addition to reflecting Humbert's perversion, Quilty reflects Humbert's strategy of combatting his enemies with laughter. Humbert thinks that by smiling at his own actions and by persuading the reader to smile, he will be able to overcome any objections to his behavior. Humbert notes that Quilty's "genre, his type of humor . . . had affinities with my own" (251). Quilty's genre is comedy, and he uses Humbert's techniques in an effort to defeat him. Instead of taking Humbert's murder threat seriously, Quilty tries to turn it into a joke or an esthetic experience. When Humbert hands Quilty an Eliotic poem explaining his motives for killing him, Quilty absurdly turns it into an exercise in literary criticism. "Well, sir, this is certainly a fine poem. Your best as far as I am concerned" (302). Undercut by the comedy, Humbert is unable to shoot; the gun goes limp in his hands. If Quilty can't turn the whole scene into a joke, he can perhaps turn it into a play, using art, as Humbert would, to save himself. Quilty is, after all, the real artist, having written numerous plays, while Humbert is merely an impostor. "I am a playwright. I have written tragedies, comedies, fantasies," Quilty argues in an effort to persuade Humbert to let him write the final scenario, since he is more experienced (300). When Humbert does manage to shoot the playwright, Quilty combines his efforts, turning the scene into a comic play, parodying Shakespeare. "Ah, that hurts, sir, enough! Ah, that hurts atrociously, my dear fellow. I pray you, desist" (305).

Quilty's comic doubling of Humbert reflects Humbert's perversion and his efforts to turn his experience into comedy or art; the structural doubling exposes Humbert's obsessions and pretensions in ways he doesn't perceive. A final example of Nabokov's parody is evident in the ending of the novel. While Humbert's novel ends with the marriage and promise of continuity typical of romance comedy, and with the expulsion and conversion of the blocking figure typical of satiric comedy, Nabokov's novel ends rather differently. In Nabokov's parody of the comic ending, Humbert dies of a coronary thrombosis, and Lolita and her daughter die in childbed. The deaths have been overlooked by some readers because they are announced at the beginning rather than the end of the novel. Other readers have argued that the deaths make the novel tragic. But the novel is not tragic; it is parodic. If Lolita, her child, and Humbert die in a parody of the comic ending, society, as represented by John Ray, Jr., and the reader, goes on. The fact that it is a humorous society merely reinforces the parody.

The final question to be answered is the one mockingly posed by Nabokov himself: "What is the author's purpose," or, more precisely, what is the effect of parodying the comic form? To answer this question we must look more closely at the technique of parody. Dorothy Van Ghent's definition of parody is a good description of Nabokov's method in *Lolita,* and it is worth quoting at length. Referring to *Don Quixote,* she observes:

> In so complex a world of contrasts, there must be something more at stake than the "right" and the "wrong" of certain ways of thinking and modes of behavior. . . . The contrasts pile up in too great a multitude for any pragmatic moral theory to keep them rigidly systematized; and the contrasted terms do not always form themselves as an occasion for acts of judgment, on the reader's part, between "right" and "wrong" or "true" and "false," but play freely among hundreds of antithetical relationships. . . .
>
> . . . Loosely, we tend to mean by parody a burlesque imitation of something, showing the weaknesses or falsehood of the object imitated. In this sense, the main feature of parody would be not unlike the main feature of debate, implying that one view of things was a "wrong" view and another the "right" view. . . . But it is possible for parody to be much more complex than debate. Instead of confronting two opposing views with each other, in order that a decision between them be arrived at, parody is able to intertwine many feelings and attitudes together in such a way that they do not merely grapple with each other antagonistically but act creatively on each other, establishing new syntheses of feeling and stimulating more comprehensive and more subtle perceptions. Parody . . . offers a field for the joyful exercise of perception and not a platform for derision.[29]

By using parody to invert the reader's expectations several times in the course of *Lolita,* Nabokov manages to achieve the complex expansion of perception that Van Ghent describes. The reader presumably begins *Lolita* with a moral scheme that rejects a disgusting pervert like Humbert Humbert. Then Humbert, with the help of John Ray, convinces the reader to shift his moral perspective and accept Humbert, perhaps even to admire him for his artistry and love. By the end of the novel, however, the reader who has inverted his moral scheme has himself become the butt of the joke. Having held two antithetical attitudes toward Humbert, total rejection and complete admiration, the reader perceives the fragility and tenuousness of moral schemes in general. The result is a more complex moral scheme, which can balance opposites and increase one's capacity for compassion. In this way parody becomes for Nabokov what it was for Sebastian Knight: "a kind of springboard for leaping into the highest region of serious emotion."[30]

Further, in parodying comic form, Nabokov is also mocking the assumptions inherent in that form. One basic assumption of comedy is that by ridiculing and reforming folly, represented by the aberrant individual, society can renew itself and celebrate its continuity. Through parody, Nabokov ridicules such an easy solution. For one thing, it is absurd to hope to improve society by excluding or converting the aberrant individual because, as Humbert demonstrates, everyone is an aberrant individual. Thus, in parodying comedy, Nabokov is parodying the didactic Meredithian theory of improvement through ridicule. Another tacit assumption of comedy is expressed in the moral of Quilty's play, "that mirage and reality merge in love" (203). It is too late in the game, Nabokov seems to be saying, to rely on such simplistic notions of the power of love.

But the virtue of parody is that it can ridicule a form or an idea while at the same time *using* that form or idea. With parody you can have it both ways. A parody of romance comedy uses the conventions of romance; a parody of satiric comedy uses the methods of satire; a parody of love and art uses the concepts of love and art. Parody has the unique capability of simultaneously ridiculing and celebrating the form and assumptions of its original. The effect is one of infinite complication. Humbert's claims of artistry and love are comically balanced by Nabokov's exposure of perversion and lust.

It is impossible, finally, to choose one view over the other. Revising and expanding our conventional notions of morality and art, Nabokov's parody forces the reader to hold all the contradictory impulses in mind at the same time. That is some trick indeed.

A parody of the Meredithian comic spirit and the Shakespearean romance hero, Humbert Humbert pretends to Todd's ironic self-knowledge and to Skipper's humorous innocence, compassion, and love. If Humbert fails in his effort to combine the opposing comic types, McMurphy and Bromden, the protagonists of Ken Kesey's *One Flew Over the Cuckoo's Nest*, succeed. Faced with an institutionalized version of the absurdity, hate, lust, and violence that characterize the humorous societies of *The Floating Opera*, *Second Skin*, and *Lolita*, McMurphy manages to combine head and heart, using laughter as a weapon against sterility and death. Although McMurphy succeeds where Humbert fails, he nevertheless suffers Humbert's fate and dies at the end of the novel. But if McMurphy dies, by the end of the novel the inmates have set themselves free, and Bromden, McMurphy's disciple and the book's real comic hero, has escaped the humorous institution to dedicate himself to life. Reaching back to the sources of comedy itself, Kesey affirms the power of laughter to free and renew the human spirit.

V.

What Laughter Can Do: Ken Kesey's One Flew Over the Cuckoo's Nest

Although Ken Kesey's *One Flew Over the Cuckoo's Nest* has been a highly successful first novel, a popular school textbook, an off-Broadway play, and a celebrated film, it has met with some rather strong criticism. The book has been charged with harboring "sexist" assumptions, portraying women as malignant "ball-cutters" or shallow "twitches," in a world gone wrong as a result of men having lost their "machismo." Marcia L. Falk, for example, assuming that the theme of the novel is the restoration of traditional male values to modern society, complains of "the psychic disease out of which the book's vision was born," insisting that the book, which purports to oppose conditioning, is "a dangerous piece of conditioning itself. With a pseudo-radical posture, it swallows whole hog all the worst attitudes toward women prevalent in our society and delivers the pig right back to us, suitably decorated and made righteous."[1] Similarly, at least one high-school board of education banned the book from the classroom on the grounds that it was racist, depicting blacks as rather ugly caricatures of evil.[2]

Such charges are not altogether misdirected; the book does treat most of its characters as caricatures, and women and blacks are cast in consistently negative roles. Raymond M. Olderman, in his excellent study of the recent American novel, reflects such misgivings about Kesey's method of simplification. According to Olderman, Kesey's "flat portrayal of women and of blacks is more stereotypic and uncomfortable than funny or fitting with his cartoon character pattern. It borders too much on the simplistic."[3]

Further, critics have not only questioned the book's treatment of women and blacks; they have also been dissatisfied with the hero, McMurphy, and with the "solution" he seems to offer to the horrors of modern life. Bruce E. Wallis, for example, argues that "the doctrine he formulated in theory cannot be effected in practice. . . . One is not bound . . . to suppose that such self-indulgence will have in reality the same meritorious outcome that it can be manipulated to achieve in art."[4] Indeed, Mc-

Murphy's "program" of fighting and fucking, of violence and sex, is as potentially manipulative as Big Nurse's shock therapy and lobotomy. The dictums to "enjoy" and "be free" can be as repressive and constricting as the dictum to conform. If mandatory muscle and wholehearted whoring is Kesey's plan for survival, then it is admittedly too simplistic, as well as utterly impracticable in real life.

Such criticisms of the novel, however, are based on two faulty assumptions: first, that the novel is a romance, and second, that McMurphy is its hero, fully embodying its values. It is important to recognize that the book is not a romance; it is a comedy. Also, McMurphy does not ultimately embody the book's comic values; Chief Bromden does.

It is perhaps not surprising that most critics read the novel as a romance. It is, after all, structured on the typical romantic antitheses: the self versus society, the human versus the mechanical, emotion versus reason, primitive versus civilized, freedom versus control, heart versus mind. McMurphy, a fascinating character, is seemingly the embodiment of Good in opposition to the Big Nurse's Evil. The plot focuses on the conflict between the Nurse's fixed pattern, unbreakable routine, and submission of the individual will to mechanical, humorless control, and McMurphy's freedom, self-reliance, and Dionysian revelry. In the course of the novel, Good finally subdues Evil, and although McMurphy loses his life, most of the inmates in the asylum go free, their health and vitality restored.

The novel, then, is structured on the kind of oppositions present in romance, and the final triumph of McMurphy over the Big Nurse seems that of nature over civilization, man over machine, emotion over reason. But the book's structural devices are finally more typical of comedy than of romance. The struggle between McMurphy and the Big Nurse is consistently portrayed in comic terms, and the final wisdom of the book is that of high comedy.

The most obvious comic devices in the novel are the reversal of expectation and the inversion of values, and the most obvious reversal is that of the human and the mechanical. According to Henri Bergson, comedy results when the mechanical is encrusted on the living; this happens throughout Kesey's novel. From the outset, people become things, and things take on a malevolent life of their own. The Big Nurse is described as made of plastic and enamel, her fingernails glowing like soldering irons. The black orderlies, her hand-picked extensions, are constantly seen in mechanical terms. According to Chief Bromden, the book's narrator, "they got special sensitive equipment detects my fear and they all look up, all three at once, eyes glittering out of the black faces like the hard glitter of radio tubes out of the back of an old radio."[5] Similarly, Doc Spivey, the ward doctor, is ruled by the inanimate. When his glasses twist askew he must tilt himself to fit them, rather than straightening them to fit him. Bromden perceives how the imposition of machines on humans renders people comic when he notes that the ward reflects "that blue-steel clarity again, that clean orderly movement of a cartoon comedy" (34).

The reversal of people and machines is, however, but one of several comic reversals that structure the book. Male and female roles are comically reversed. If men have traditionally oppressed women, now the women oppress the men. In the asylum, the weak, ineffectual men are controlled by strong, domineering women, rendering the sexual roles themselves comic. Indeed, Kesey takes the worst male stereotype available—that of overweening power, control, force, manipulation—and imposes it on the women in the book, and the worst female stereotype—pettiness, bitchiness, lack of self-confidence, anxiousness to serve—and imposes it on the men. Thus, thirty-one-year-old Billy Bibbit remains his mother's weak, effeminate child; Harding, embarrassed by his lovely hands, is rendered impotent by his sexually demanding wife; and Chief Bromden's father "shrinks" when his wife muscles him out of his land and his heritage. The Big Nurse, of course, comically reflects them all in her paternalistic attitude and disguised aggression toward her patients. Although McMurphy admits that he couldn't "get it up" over the Nurse, Harding notes in a telling pun that the Nurse "eventually gets inside everyone" (70).

Just as the traditional male–female roles are reversed, so are the traditional black–white roles. Whereas the blacks were traditionally the slaves of white masters, now the whites are the slaves of black masters, and Washington, named for the father and capital of our free country, is their leader.

To fault Kesey for his treatment of women and blacks is to miss the comedy of a device that has informed comic art from Aristophanes to Erica Jong, the reversal of traditional roles. In our day the traditional roles have themselves become grotesquely comic; their reversal compounds the comedy.

The reversal of human and mechanical, and of traditional male–female and black–white roles, is a comic indication that the world is out of joint. The motive force behind all these reversals is, according to Bromden, the Combine, the social structure that threshes and levels individuals, turning them into caricatures. The microcosm of this malign social structure is the institution, and Nurse Ratched's ward in particular. Indeed, the discrepancy between the institution's official image and its actual practice provides some of the blackest comedy in the book. The PR man who pops up periodically best articulates the institution's view of itself. Himself a figure of fun, with a "face bloated up red and round as a balloon with a face painted on it" (35) and a body "like a rubber toy—if you push him over he's weighted on the bottom and straightaway rocks back upright, goes to spinning again" (36), PR rhapsodizes on the progress made by his institution. "Oh, when I think back on the old days, on the filth, the bad food, even, yes, brutality, oh, I realize, ladies, that we have come a long way in our campaign!" (9). PR's catalogue of horrors fairly accurately, if unintentionally, describes his own institution. According to the Chief, the patients stand in their own urine and eat shit "chewed thirty-two times apiece by the stainless-steel machine in the kitchen. I see it purse sectioned lips, like a vacuum-cleaner hose, and spurt a clot of chewed-up ham onto a plate with a barnyard sound" (30). The "Disposable Not To Be Re-Used" catheter sacks are washed nightly by the Chief for use on the Chronics, whose legs have been ripped clean of hair by repeated applications of tape (31). Further, if the orderlies are prevented from disciplining the patients with socks filled with buckshot as they would prefer, they are taught equally effective methods by the Big Nurse. Her methods culminate in such humanitarian techniques as shock treatments and lobotomies, which result in cures like Ruckley's, his eyes "all smoked up and gray and deserted inside like blown fuses," and Taber's, who goes "wandering round in a simple, happy dream. A success" (15–16). For all the institution's claims, it is obvious that the methods employed to "help" the patients do more to keep them maladjusted, or adjusted so well that they cease to be human. In its comic ignorance, the institution cannot even recognize Santa Claus, preferring to commit him, shave him, and thin him down over a six-year period so that he may return to a functional existence in the Combine (73).

It becomes increasingly apparent in the course of the novel that the inmates, who are supposed to be sick, are really healthy, and the Combine, which is supposed to be healthy, is really sick. What the men learn from McMurphy is that they are "not any crazier than the average asshole on the street"; in fact, they may be less so (63). The doctor, on the other hand, is "a little slow in the head" (60), while the Big Nurse, according to one of her own colleagues, is "a little sick" herself (266). The reversal of sanity and insanity is, then, a final comic device structuring the novel and exposing the humorous society.

Kesey's metaphor for this society is the institution, and the emblem of the institution is the Big Nurse. As representative of the humorously mechanical society, Nurse Ratched resembles the archetypal comic villain.[6] Like the typical villain of traditional comedy, the Big Nurse is a boastful impostor and self-deceived pedant who pretends to know more than she does. She is the obsessed antagonist who tries to force the plot of the novel into compliance with her own comic delusions and who, in the end, must be defeated or expelled if the comic values of life and continuity are to be celebrated. She recalls the comic doctors of Molière and the pedants of Fielding and Pope, but she more closely resembles the villains of recent comic fiction. Like Nabokov's Clare Quilty, Hawkes's Miranda and Tremlow, and Coover's Horace Zifferblatt, for example, she is an extreme personification of her humorous society, her very excesses rendering her comic. Disturbed by the "permissive philosophy" of modern mental hospitals, the Nurse manages to maintain the old brutalities in modern disguise. Substituting subtle psychological cruelties for physical punishment, she succeeds in debilitating the men mentally and spiritually, in persuading them of their inadequacy. By pretending concern and affection for her patients, she manipulates their fears and anxieties, slowly destroying any self-confidence or respect they may have had, torturing them on the rack of allusion and insinuation.

Like the comic villains mentioned above, the Big Nurse is powerful and destructive, but she is also finally unable to destroy the comic values and assumptions implicit in the novel. By treating the Nurse as a caricature of evil, Kesey controls and tempers her power, allowing Chief Bromden and several other inmates to escape, healthy and intact, from the control of the Combine. In the course of the novel, as in most comedy, her obsessions turn back on her. Although she destroys McMurphy's body, she is unable to destroy his spirit or meaning, and, at the end, she is exhausted and depleted.

Her very name is a joke, qualifying her omnipotence. McMurphy punningly calls her Miss Rat-shed (93); her name also rather neatly suggests both her nature and her fate: wretched. Further, like a ratchet wrench she keeps her patients "adjusted," but like a ratchet, a gear in the Combine, she is herself mechanically enmeshed. Personifiying the Combine, she is responsible for the very mechanical symbols that ultimately render her comic. Early in the novel, when she gets mad at her orderlies, the Chief notes, "She's swelling up, swells till her back's splitting out the white uniform and she's let her arms section out long enough to wrap around the three of them five, six times. . . . and she blows up bigger and bigger, big as a tractor, so big I can smell the machinery inside" (4–5). Later, the Chief pictures her "in the center of this web of wires like a watchful robot, tend her network with mechanical insect skill" (26).

Although the machine imagery intensifies the horror of the control symbolized by the Nurse, it deflates her as well. If the Nurse is a machine, she can be short-circuited or turned off; she can be defeated. It's only a matter of finding the switch or figuring out the wiring pattern, something McMurphy is ultimately able to do. Indeed, the Big Nurse in many ways becomes a kind of comic-strip villain, a mechanical genius who tries to defeat the superhero by means of her technology and scientific knowhow. As in the typical comic-book plot, she is defeated by a hero who uses only his natural cunning and personal strength.

If, as is typical of the comic *alazon*, the Nurse helps to defeat herself, the machine turning on its creator, McMurphy is significantly responsible for her defeat, and he adopts several roles in an effort to unplug or short-circuit her. One of the Nurse's main weaknesses is her lack of a sense of humor, her inability to see what the Chief refers to as the "funny side to things" (227). This is perhaps the most significant thematic distinction between McMurphy and the Nurse. While the Nurse's smile is chiseled or painted on her plastic face, McMurphy's laughter is genuine and all-encompassing. Laughter is McMurphy's most effective weapon, and in his role as laugher he resembles Meredith's comic spirit or the traditional comic *eiron*.

The first thing McMurphy notices when he appears on the ward as a new admission is the absence of laughter. Although the men often "snicker in their fists, . . . nobody ever dares let loose and laugh" (14). According to the Chief, the institution itself prevents it: "The air is pressed in by the walls, too tight for laughing" (46). Indeed, the whole book is in some ways a vision of a world without laughter, and it is McMurphy's job to restore laughter, and thus health, to this sterile, humorless world. McMurphy explains, "I haven't heard a real laugh since I came through that door, do you know that? Man, when you lose your laugh you lose your *footing*" (68). If McMurphy hasn't heard a laugh since he arrived on the ward, the Chief has, for the first thing McMurphy does upon entering is laugh. Bromden notes, "When nobody makes a move to say anything to him he commences to laugh. Nobody can tell exactly why he laughs; there's nothing funny going on. But it's not the way that Public Relation laughs, it's free and loud and it comes out of his wide grinning mouth and spreads in rings bigger and bigger till it's lapping against the walls all over the ward. . . . This sounds real. I realize all of a sudden it's the first laugh I've heard in years. . . . Even when he isn't laughing, that laughing sound hovers around him" (11). When McMurphy laughs, "dials twitch in the control panel at the sound of it," indicating, early in the novel, that the Combine is beatable and that the appropriate weapon is laughter (17).

Teaching the men to laugh is no easy problem, however, for it involves making them see their own inherent comedy; they must learn to laugh at themselves as well as at their situation. In a world without laughter, the inmates are suspicious of McMurphy, whose "big wide-open laugh" makes everyone uneasy (17). Initially unable to appreciate McMurphy's sense of humor, the patients label him a boastful impostor, a manipulator. Harding dismisses him as "cowboy bluster," and "sideshow swagger" (64), calling him "a backwoods braggart" (56). Indeed, McMurphy is partly in the tradition of the boaster and braggart, the backwoods teller of tall tales common in nineteenth-century American humor. Brash con man and swaggering gambler, he descends upon the ward as if he, and not the Nurse, owned it. But it's soon clear to the patients and the reader that McMurphy's boasting is, unlike the Nurse's, a consciously adopted comic pose, indicating his perception of the comedy of things. Whereas the Nurse always takes herself very solemnly, McMurphy rarely fails to see his own human comedy. In his first conversation with Harding, he boasts that he has been a bull goose catskinner, gambler, and pea weeder, and now "if I'm bound to be a loony, then I'm bound to be a stompdown dadgum good one" (19). Parodying his own role of cowboy hero, McMurphy tells Harding that the ward isn't big enough for both of them and that Harding must either meet him "man to man or he's a yaller skunk and better be outta town by sunset" (19). McMurphy wins the lunacy contest that follows, by claiming that he's so crazy that he plans to vote for Eisenhower, *again* (20). Throughout the novel McMurphy couches his boasts in humor, revealing his comic perspective of himself. Although he places great importance on his sexual virility, for example, he "'boasts" that a nine-year-old girl originally stole his virginity. "She got to where she was tripping me and beating me to the floor" (43). Like Barth's Todd Andrews, Hawkes's Skipper, and Nabokov's Humbert Humbert, McMurphy is "raped" by a female, rather than him raping her.

McMurphy knows that when a person "can't laugh any more . . . he loses one of the biggest edges he's got on his side" (68). But merely laughing is not in itself enough. PR laughs, and Doc Spivey laughs, and their laughter is ineffectual. What McMurphy learns in the course of the novel is how to control and direct his laughter, how to use it as an effective counter to repression and sterility. What he really learns, and nearly masters, is the typical pose of the comic spirit.

The typical comic plot, as I have noted, is structured as a conflict of two archetypal characters, the *alazon* and the *eiron*. If the Nurse is the boastful impostor and self-deceived fool, McMurphy becomes the witty self-deprecator who pretends ignorance in an effort to defeat his opponent, to bring her to confusion. Although McMurphy's natural tendency is to use violence or virility to subdue people, his profession as con man has admirably prepared him for the role of *eiron*. As a "good old red, white, and blue hundred-per-cent American con man" McMurphy knows the virtue of pretending ignorance to take people in (254). Thus he pretends to lose card games at low stakes so that he can entice others to lose at higher stakes. It is this kind of strategy that proves ultimately most successful against the Big Nurse. Perceiving that the Big Nurse is literally impregnable and that her technology will always be stronger than his own physical prowess, McMurphy bets the inmates that he will be able to defeat the Nurse by adopting the *eiron*'s pose (70–71). The Chief explains McMurphy's strategy. "A couple of times some stupid rule gets him mad, but he just makes himself act more polite and mannerly than ever till he begins to see how funny the whole thing is—the rules, the disapproving looks they use to enforce the rules, the ways of talking to you like you're nothing but a three-year-old—and when he sees how funny it is he goes to laughing, and this aggravates them no end. He's safe as long as he can laugh, he thinks, and it works pretty fair" (113). Pretending to be unaffected by the Nurse's manipulations, McMurphy effectively short-circuits them.

The teeth-brushing episode is McMurphy's first victory over the Nurse. When McMurphy questions the ward policy of locking up the toothpaste and unlocking it at a specific time only, the black attendant absurdly insists, "What you s'pose it'd be like if *evahbody* was to brush their teeth whenever they took a notion to brush? . . . My *gaw*, don't you see?" Instead of reacting hostilely, McMurphy enthusiastically agrees, his very agreement ridiculing the rule and the attendant. "Yes, now, I do. You're saying people'd be brushin' their teeth whenever the spirit moved them. . . . And, lordy, can you imagine? Teeth bein' brushed at six-thirty, six-twenty—who can tell? maybe even six o'clock. Yeah, I can see your point" (90). Prepared for a fight, the attendant doesn't know how to respond to McMurphy's agreement" and retreats.

McMurphy then uses a similar strategy on the Nurse. When she approaches, "her lips are parted, and her smile's going out before her like a radiator grill . . . and every step hits the floor she blows up a size bigger" (93). But McMurphy, apparently dressed only in his cap and a towel, is as polite as can be, pretending ignorance and full cooperation. When she asks him where his clothes are, he sadly replies in all innocence that they were stolen. The Nurse is confused until she realizes that "that outfit was *supposed* to be picked up" and McMurphy should be wearing his hospital "greens," not a towel. McMurphy apologizes and obligingly begins to remove the towel, flustering the Nurse into commanding him to leave it on. McMurphy pretends confusion and redirects the Nurse's anger against the attendant, an extension of herself, by insisting that he neglected to issue McMurphy a uniform. McMurphy crowns his victory by casually removing the towel to reveal his black-with-white-whales undershorts, ridiculing the Nurse's fear that he was naked underneath. Using the *eiron*'s methods of pretended ignorance and self-deprecation, McMurphy defeats the *alazon*, turning the Nurse's humorlessness against her.

The book is filled with similar, smaller examples of McMurphy's strategy. In the group therapy sessions, he pretends to worry about his excessive sexual appetite, prodding a laugh out of Doc Spivey (44). Several times he "forgets" about the glass in the Nurse's station and runs his hand through it. When the Nurse criticizes his failure to clean the toilets properly, insisting, "This is an outrage," he replies politely, "No; that's a toilet bowl" (151). McMurphy's program gives the men at least a partial appreciation of the comedy of their situation, enabling them to act for the first time in years. When the Nurse refuses to allow them to watch the World Series on TV, they all sit down with McMurphy to watch the blank screen, indicating their progress toward health and a comic understanding. The Chief remarks, "If somebody'd of come in and took a look, men watching a blank TV, a fifty-year-old woman hollering and squealing at the back of their heads about discipline and order and recriminations, they'd of thought the whole bunch was crazy as loons" (138).

McMurphy's first strategy for helping the patients is that of the comic *eiron*: pretended ignorance and wise laughter. But McMurphy eventually moves beyond humor to myth, reflecting the primitive origins of comedy itself. Most scholars now agree that comedy is an outgrowth of certain ancient rituals and fertility rites. *One Flew Over the Cuckoo's Nest* is virtually structured on the four elements of the fertility ritual F. M. Cornford describes in *The Origin of Attic Comedy*: the carrying out of death and the subsequent renewal of life; the fight of summer and winter, a seasonal antagonism that must end in the victory of summer over the sterility of winter; the struggle between the young king and the old; and death and resurrection, which are often imaged in the dismemberment and rebirth of a god.[7] In the novel, the Chief and the other inmates suffer a ritual death, witness the fight between the cold, white Big Nurse and the warm, redheaded Irishman, and are finally freed to new life through McMurphy's symbolic dismemberment and the Nurse's symbolic death. Wylie Sypher notes that "from the earliest time the comic ritual has been presided over by a Lord of Misrule, and the improvisations of comedy have the aspect of a Feast of Unreason, a Revel of Fools."[8] In his effort to restore humor to the men's lives, McMurphy adopts this role of Lord of Misrule, bringing the festivity and revelry of ancient ritual to the ward.

The first element of revelry McMurphy brings to the ward is, of course, laughter. For the Lord of Misrule, laughter is aggressive, a substitute for actual physical attack. As Sypher notes, the Greeks used laughter "to express a disdain roused by seeing someone's mischance, deformity, or ugliness. . . . To be laughed at by the ancients was to be defiled."[9] Morton Gurewitch observes that laughter can be "a laudable equivalent for direct physical assault."[10] But McMurphy's laughter seems to have another function as well, a function that is perhaps best stated in Freudian terms. For Freudians, laughter is an upsurge from the unconscious, releasing powerful archaic impulses. Laughter celebrates and frees the irrational as a means of countering the repressive demands of the superego.[11] In *One Flew Over the Cuckoo's Nest*, laughter releases repressed energies in the patients, helping them to recover a portion of their atrophied instinctual lives. The Chief, for example, regains his senses:

> I get a smell of something that makes me realize for the first time since I been in the hospital that this big dorm full of beds, sleeps forty grown men, has always been sticky with a thousand other smells—smells of germicide, zinc ointment, and foot powder, smell of piss and sour old-man manure, of Pablum and eyewash, of musty shorts and socks musty even when they're fresh back from the laundry, the stiff odor of starch in the linen, the acid stench of morning mouths, the banana smell of machine oil, and sometimes the smell of singed hair. (97–98)

Bromden thus notices, for the first time, the institutional smells with which he lives. Later he rediscovers the smells of nature. Having refused to take his tranquilizers one evening, he sneaks out of bed and gazes into the moonlight.

> The wire was cold and sharp, and I rolled my head against it from side to side to feel it with my cheeks, and I smelled the breeze. It's fall coming, I thought, I can smell that sour-molasses smell of silage, clanging the air like a bell—smell somebody's been burning oak leaves, left them to smolder overnight because they're too green.
>
> It's fall coming, I kept thinking, fall coming; just like that was the strangest thing ever happened. Fall. Right outside here it was spring a while back, then it was summer, and now it's fall—that's sure a curious idea. (154–55)

Having recovered his instinctual life, Bromden recalls the ritual change of seasons, winter inevitably giving way to spring.

Since McMurphy's laughter is in part directed toward the recovery of the instinctual life, it is appropriate that his jokes should be sexual or scatological. As Lord of Misrule, presiding over a fertility ritual, McMurphy resembles such sexual comedians as Gay's Captain Macheath, Fielding's Tom Jones, and Henry Miller's persona in *The Tropic of Cancer.* In one group therapy session, for example, the men discuss Harding's difficulty in coping with his wife's large breasts. When the Nurse ignorantly asks if anyone wants "to touch upon this subject further," McMurphy gleefully raises his hand (42). Later in the book he delights in taping dirty jokes written in mirror language to the undersides of the toilet bowls for the Nurse's inspection.

But McMurphy does not use jokes and laughter alone to restore instinctual life to the ward. According to Freud, alcohol and sex are even more effective restoratives, and McMurphy is quite prepared to oblige. On the fishing trip the Chief drinks four cans of beer, "shorting out dozens of control leads down inside me" (235). The very presence of Candy, a prostitute, on the ward is enough to short-circuit it. Bromden notes that "apparatus burned out all over the ward trying to adjust to her come busting in like she did—took electronic readings on her and calculated they weren't built to handle something like this on the ward, and just burned out, like machines committing suicide" (219). The idea of machines taking on enough life to commit suicide is itself, of course, comic. Finally, McMurphy's singing, like his laughter, his booze, and his sexuality, is capable of "joggling the wiring in all the walls" (88).

As a Dionysian Lord of Misrule, McMurphy thus presides over a comic fertility ritual, restoring instinctual life to the patients. Wylie Sypher remarks that "if the authentic comic action is a sacrifice and a feast, debate and passion, it is by the same token a Saturnalia, an orgy, an assertion of the unruliness of the flesh and its vitality."[12] The final orgy in the book represents a culmination of the sexuality, drunkenness, vitality, and laughter represented by McMurphy. Mixing wine and cough syrup, and thus using the Combine's own resources as part of the revelry, the men get drunk; Billy Bibbit and Candy participate in a mock wedding ceremony, celebrating the loss of Billy's virginity; Sefelt combines an epileptic seizure with sexual intercourse, turning debility to power and causing Sandy to marvel, "I never experienced anything like it" (290); Chief Bromden manages to laugh in the very heart of the Combine, persuading him that "maybe the Combine wasn't all-powerful. What was to stop us from doing it again, now that we saw we could?" (292). Finally, when the Big Nurse appears on the scene, the men retain their ability to laugh. "Every laugh was being forced right down her throat till it looked as if any minute she'd blow up like a bladder" (297). "The men were immune to her poison. Their eyes met hers; their grins mocked the old confident smile she had lost" (299).

Thus McMurphy adopts two comic roles in battling the Nurse: the *eiron*'s pretended ignorance and comic perspective and the Lord of Misrule's laughter and revelry. But his commitment to the men ultimately precludes the kind of detachment necessary for a true *eiron* or Lord of Misrule, and his participation in an ancient comic ritual necessitates his sacrifice. Even in his third role, that of sacrificial redeemer, however, he remains deeply comic.

As Wylie Sypher suggests, the story of Christ, sometimes mistaken for a tragedy, is really a comedy. "The drama of the struggle, death, and rising—Gethsemane, Calvary, and Easter—actually belongs in the comic rather than the tragic domain. The figure of Christ as god-man is surely the archetypal hero-victim."[13] In his role as Christ figure, McMurphy thus parodies a comedy, the Christian drama inherent in the plot rendering the novel at once more comic and more serious. If McMurphy is a parody of Christ, he nonetheless reflects Christ's meaning and values.

Although allusions to the Christian story occur throughout the novel, the three episodes that most clearly reflect parallels are the fishing trip, the shock therapy, and the orgy. Midway in the book, McMurphy manages to persuade ten patients, along with Candy and Doc Spivey, to accompany him on a salmon-fishing trip. The symbolism is overt. First, Ellis, the Chronic nailed to the wall, pulls his hands down for a moment and advises Billy Bibbit to be a "fisher of men" (222). Then Chief Bromden notes with appropriately biblical intonation, "McMurphy led the twelve of us toward the ocean" (227). Finally, the fish, an obvious symbol of fertility, is also the traditional symbol of Christianity.

On board the fishing boat, the men drink and cavort, and even catch fish. But the single most important consequence of the trip is the restoration of the men's sense of humor. If McMurphy can't walk on water like his predecessor, his laughter can, and it's laughter that ultimately saves the men. The Chief describes McMurphy "spreading his laugh out across the water," laughing "because he knows you have to laugh at the things that hurt you just to keep yourself in balance, just to keep the world from running you plumb crazy. He knows there's a painful side; he knows my thumb smarts and his girl friend has a bruised breast and the doctor is losing his glasses, but he won't let the pain blot out the humor no more'n he'll let the humor blot out the pain" (237–38). When the men begin to laugh, it's no longer just amusement at McMurphy's antics, it's laughter "at their own selves as well as at the rest of us" (238). Seeing their own weaknesses and failures in a comic perspective, they are practically cured.

If the fishing excursion invigorates the men, it depletes McMurphy, who begins to appear like the man of sorrows. Obviously suffering from the strain of infusing his own life into others, McMurphy is "beat and worn out" (243), "dreadfully tired and strained and *frantic*, like there wasn't enough time left for something he had to do . . ." (245). What he has to do, of course, is complete the role of redeemer by dying for the men, and the shock treatments he subsequently receives comically parallel the crucifixion. Early in the book, Harding describes the shock treatments: "You are strapped to a table, shaped, ironically, like a cross, with a crown of electric sparks in place of thorns" (67). Once inside the shock shop, McMurphy himself humorously perceives his role. "Anointest my head with conductant," he intones. "Do I get a crown of thorns?" (270). Another patient adopts the role of Pilate, insisting, "I wash my hands of the whole deal" (264), but it is finally the Big Nurse who completes that role, offering McMurphy the same deal Pilate offered Christ. If he will recant, if he will "*admit* he was wrong," then the "treatment would be canceled" (268). McMurphy characteristically refuses, and the mock crucifixion continues.

The mock crucifixion does not, however, prevent McMurphy from participating in the prearranged orgy, a kind of Last Supper, complete with wine, prayer, and betrayal. Drunkenly blessing the union of Billy Bibbit and Candy, Harding intones, "Most merciful God, accept these two poor sinners into your arms. And keep the doors ajar for the coming of the rest of us, because you are witnessing the end" (291). The end comes the morning after the orgy when the Big Nurse uses her powerful weapon of guilt on Billy Bibbit, forcing him, like Judas, to betray his savior and commit suicide. Faced with the inevitable, McMurphy, like Christ, "gave a cry. . . . he let himself cry out: A sound of cornered-animal fear and hate . . . when he finally doesn't care any more about anything but himself and his dying" (305). Ultimately McMurphy is crucified on the lobotomy table, and the Chief's final dialogue with Scanlon has the appropriate biblical ring:

> "Is it finished?"
> I told him yeah.
> "Christ, he said then." (309)

But, of course, it isn't finished any more than Christianity was finished when Christ was crucified. In a sense it has just begun. Earlier, McMurphy had blown the Chief back up to size by "transmitting his own blood" into him (24). At the end, Bromden participates in a comic communion, partaking of McMurphy's body by killing it. The Chief escapes to become McMurphy's biographer, and, as the participants in the orgiastic Last Supper would all agree, "it's every word gospel" (297).

The Christian parallels have led one critic to claim that "the novel is expressly formulated as nothing less than the bible for a twentieth-century religion of self-assertive action, with a message of salvation modulated to the needs of repressed individuals in a constrictively conformist society."[14] If the novel is something less than that, it does reflect the kind of affirmation and hope symbolized by the life, death, and resurrection of Christ, and it does argue for individual freedom and action. At the end, the Nurse and the repressive institution she symbolizes are shrunken and impotent, and the inmates, with a renewed sense of the funny side of things, have released themselves from the asylum.

But the novel is not quite so simple. The conflict is not so clearly one between pure good and pure evil. McMurphy is not merely a hero, he is a comic hero, and like other comic heroes, he reveals a decided ambivalence.[15] As I noted at the outset, readers have criticized McMurphy (and Kesey) for his attitude toward women and blacks, for his aggressive sexuality, and for his conviction that the irrational, the chaotic, the Dionysian, must triumph over the rational, the ordered, the Apollonian. Assuming that Kesey intended McMurphy as an ideal model of healthy manhood, these readers have found Kesey's vision to be disappointing, his solution to the problems of the contemporary world impracticable and simplistic. But it is possible that Kesey himself was aware of McMurphy's shortcomings and that he intended them as a means of undercutting McMurphy, ultimately directing reader attention away from McMurphy to the more adequate embodiment of the book's comic philosophy, Chief Bromden, the author of the novel. Perhaps when a critic like Robert Boyers complains that "we are never quite certain whether to laugh at McMurphy as well as with him,"[16] he has discovered an intentional complexity in the novel, and in McMurphy's character.

If McMurphy exposes his humorous society, he also exposes himself, both consciously and unconsciously. Like the Big Nurse, her attendants, Doc Spivey, and PR, McMurphy is deflated through caricature. If he is often depicted as a parody of Christ, he is as often described as a kind of cartoon cowboy or comic-book superhero. The inmates see him in these simplistic terms, making him "hitch up his black shorts like they were horsehide chaps, and push back his cap with one finger like it was a ten-gallon Stetson" (305). At the end of the orgy, Harding imagines seeing McMurphy off. "I'd like to stand there at the window with a silver bullet in my hand and ask 'Who *wawz* that'er masked man?' " (295). McMurphy himself boasts of his "trigger-quick mind" while exercising his intelligence by reading his favorite cartoon magazines (172, 174). The Chief has his own comic-book picture of McMurphy, envisioning him as "a giant come out of the sky to save us from the Combine" (255). Indeed, McMurphy clearly resembles the typical comic-book superhero who uses his secret powers and physical strength to defeat the evil, scientific villain.

The comparison of McMurphy to TV cowboys and comic-book superheroes in part adds to the pain and tragedy of McMurphy's role, since, unlike his make-believe counterparts, he can be hurt both emotionally and physically; it also in part elevates McMurphy, since he often consciously caricatures himself, thus revealing his comic perspective. But the comparison also serves to expose McMurphy's deficiencies. For instance, most superheroes have rather unsatisfactory sex lives, exerting their energy to protect their secret identities from prying females. Although McMurphy seems to believe that free sexuality and libidinous zest are the best answers to psychic repression, his actual sexual experiences are comically discrepant with his immodest claims. McMurphy's only sexual experience actually described in the book is one with a nine-year-old girl, who is the aggressor. Later, at the orgy, when McMurphy and Sandy fall into bed, they are "more like two tired little kids than a grown man and a grown woman in bed together to make love" (296). McMurphy's infantile sexuality is at odds with his avowed potency.

Further, McMurphy is, at times, obnoxious. He is loud and crude, imposing his way of life on people just as the Big Nurse imposes hers. He tosses beer cans out car windows, continually breaks laws, gets his way by fighting and fucking, flicks butter at walls, and openly rejects notions of quietude, reason, tolerance, and good temper. For all his good qualities, McMurphy exposes his comic deficiencies in the same way that Barth's Todd Andrews, Hawkes's Skipper, and Nabokov's Humbert Humbert do.

Finally, McMurphy's program for liberating the men is not an unqualified success. In the course of the battle with the Big Nurse, both Cheswick and Billy Bibbit, unprepared for McMurphy's tactics, commit suicide. Even more significantly, McMurphy himself loses his comic perspective at the end and becomes evil to fight evil, using his old methods of violence and virility against the Big Nurse. Robert Boyers puts it succinctly: "In his fear and frustration, he does not see what, of all things, should be most obvious to him: that he cannot make another human being aware of his humanity by destroying or suppressing those elements of his own humanity that have made McMurphy a beautiful person."[17] Indeed, McMurphy's initials, RPM, may suggest his power, but they may also suggest his futility, going around in circles, being played on the Combine's machine.

Like the typical comic hero, McMurphy exposes himself as well as his humorous society. Unlike the typical comic hero, he dies for his mistakes. At the end, trying to fight the Combine with its own dehumanizing weapons, McMurphy becomes almost a tragic figure, prompting critics like Ruth H. Brady to conclude that the novel is "anything but hopeful."[18] Indeed, if McMurphy were the only hero of the novel, alone embodying its values, the novel would be a tragedy or, perhaps, a melodrama. But McMurphy is not ultimately the hero of the book—Chief Bromden is.

It is important to remember that the ostensible author of

One Flew Over the Cuckoo's Nest is not Ken Kesey, but Chief Bromden, a schizophrenic Indian. Kesey himself regarded his inspiration to use Bromden as narrator as a major breakthrough in the writing of the novel. "Think of this: I, me ken kesey, is stepped back another step and am writing about a third person author writing about something. Fair makes the mind real [*sic*], don't it?"[19] In *One Flew Over the Cuckoo's Nest*, as in *The Floating Opera*, *Second Skin*, and *Lolita*, a novelist is writing a novel about a novelist writing a novel about his own life. Thus it is Bromden, and not necessarily Kesey, who is ultimately responsible for the creation of McMurphy. McMurphy is Bromden's romantic vision of what a hero should be like, his action and motives existing only insofar as Bromden imagines them. McMurphy becomes in part a metaphor for Bromden's own development, and the central focus of the novel is on Bromden's growth toward health and a comic understanding of himself and his society.

Chief Bromden is, after all, the only fully developed character in the book. While McMurphy, Big Nurse, and the minor characters surrounding them remain, for the most part, rather flat caricatures, Bromden, at first a caricature, changes, grows, and develops in the course of the novel, emerging at the end as a complete and strong individual. He is the only character with a past. Although we do see fragments of McMurphy's childhood, Bromden's Indian heritage and his childhood experiences are integrally related to his adult existence. In the course of the novel Bromden flashes back to various childhood memories, the most important being his encounter with the government officials, the experience that resulted in his deaf and dumb act. Not finding Bromden's father home, the government officials calmly and openly discuss their plans to steal his heritage, as if young Bromden were not even there. Bromden comments, "I remembered one thing: it wasn't me that started acting deaf; it was people that first started acting like I was too dumb to hear or see or say anything at all" (198). His experience with the government officials persuades Bromden that the only way to survive in a hostile white world is to play deaf and dumb. The strategy enables him to see and hear things he otherwise couldn't. The Big Nurse and her attendants freely expose their villainy to him since they perceive him to be no threat.

A related event from the Chief's past that has significance for the book as a whole is the conflict between his mother and father. Mrs. Bromden was a domineering woman who cared little for her husband's Indian heritage and was instrumental in selling his land to the government. As the Chief tells McMurphy, "my mother made him too little to fight any more and he gave up" (208). The Chief's childhood experience here closely parallels the plot of the novel. Just as the Chief's mother worked on his father to make him small, so the Big Nurse works on the Chief and McMurphy. Just as the government officials failed to hear or see Bromden, so the medical staff labels him deaf and dumb. In some ways the Chief's novel is a fictionalized account of his childhood experience. Thus McMurphy and the Big Nurse are not "real" characters at all, but rather the Chief's metaphors for his own "real" experience. In fictionalizing his life the Chief, like Todd Andrews, Skipper, and Humbert Humbert, becomes the comic hero of his own book, exposing both himself and his society.

From the outset, the Chief is a comic figure, the discrepancy between his paranoid delusions and the reader's view of reality accounting for much of the humor early in the book. The Chief is firmly convinced, for example, that the mythical Combine controls everything "on hair-like wires too small for anybody's eyes but mine" (26). The Chief literally sees microphones in the broom handles, wires in the walls, pernicious devices in the electric shavers, clocks that accelerate and decelerate at will. When the plastic and enamel Big Nurse gets angry with Bromden, he perceives her cramming her wicker bag down his throat with the broom handle or turning on her fog machine so that he will get lost. Similarly, according to the Chief, Ruckley's eyes are burned out, and Ellis is nailed to the wall until his urine rots the floor beneath him and he falls through to the ward below. Taken literally, the Chief's vision of things on the ward is outrageously comic.

If the Chief's image of the ward is comic, so is his self-image. Although he is actually six-foot-eight, he thinks of himself as little. He tells McMurphy, "I'm way too little. I used to be big, but not no more. You're twice the size of me" (207). Harding describes him as "a giant janitor. There's your Vanishing American, a six-foot-eight sweeping machine, scared of its own shadow" (67). The discrepancy between the Chief's self-image and his actual size can be added to the comic reversals mentioned earlier: sane and insane, male and female, people and machines, black and white.

Two additional reversals add to the Chief's comedy. First, Bromden is an Indian, and consequently a victim of race prejudice, who is himself prejudiced. The blacks are "niggers" to the Chief, forces of pure evil, malevolent machines. "If you brush against their hair," he confides solemnly, "it rasps the hide right off you" (28). If his prejudice is based on some painful firsthand experience, Bromden is nevertheless comic in the manner of Joseph Heller's Chief White Half Oat in *Catch-22*. "Racial prejudice," says that chief, "is a terrible thing, Yossarian. It really is. It's a terrible thing to treat a decent, loyal Indian like a nigger, kike, wop or spic."[20]

Second, the usual convention of the Indian and the white man in American literature is reversed. Whereas the fictional Indian, Cooper's Chingachgook and Faulkner's Sam Fathers, for example, usually introduces the white man to a way of life that goes back to nature, in Kesey's comic reversal of the myth, it takes a white man, ignorant of the land and fishing, to lead the Indian back. With a final twist on the convention, Kesey has the white man die first, while the Indian lives on. Leslie Fiedler notes, "It is the first real *Liebestod* in our long literature of love between white man and colored, and the first time, surely, that the Indian partner in such a pair has outlived his White brother. Typically, Chingachgook had predeceased Natty, and Queequeg, Ishmael; typically, Huck had been younger than Jim, Ike than Sam Fathers. Everyone who has lived at the heart of our dearest myth knows that it is the white boy-man who survives, as the old Indian, addressing the Great Spirit, prepares to vanish."[21]

Chief Bromden is thus a comic figure, the discrepancy between his vision and the reader's and the reversal of literary conventions assuring his comedy. But if the Chief is comic, he is also a hero. Since Bromden has written the novel, it is Bromden himself who exposes his own comedy. The plot traces Bromden's growth toward the kind of comic perspective that enables him to write such a novel. When he can turn the Combine into comedy, he has defeated it.

At first, Bromden sees nothing funny about the cartoon world in which he and the other inmates are trapped. The men "are flat and outlined in black, jerking through some kind of goofy story, that might be real funny if it weren't for the cartoon figures being real guys" (31). The ward, which livens up perceptibly when McMurphy enters, nevertheless soon "takes on that blue-steel clarity again, that clean orderly movement of a cartoon comedy" (34). The technicians controlling it all are themselves "like cartoon men—or like puppets, mechanical puppets in one of those Punch and Judy acts where it's supposed to be funny to see the puppet beat up by the Devil and swallowed headfirst by a smiling alligator" (35). Faced with such a humorless cartoon of a world, it is no wonder that Bromden longs for a superhero to descend from the sky to save him. But McMurphy's super powers are not what finally save the Chief; what saves him in his own sense of humor.

Bromden's development toward a comic understanding parallels McMurphy's development from *eiron* to Lord of Misrule to sacrificial redeemer. When McMurphy begins to ply the *eiron*'s strategy of pretended ignorance against the Nurse and her staff, winning the battle over the teeth brushing, Bromden recalls his father's use of a similar strategy against the government officials. When the officials originally approached Bromden's father about selling his land, he pretended not to understand, speaking instead in a parody of Indian dialect.

> "Geese up there, white man. You know it. Geese this year. And last year. And the year before and the year before."
>
> The men looked at one another and cleared their throats. "Yes. Maybe true, Chief Bromden. Now. Forget geese. Pay attention to contract. What we offer could greatly benefit you—your people—change the lives of the red man."
>
> Papa said, " . . . and the year before and the year before and the year before . . ."
>
> By the time it dawned on the government men that they were being poked fun at, all the council who'd been sitting on the porch of our shack, putting pipes in the pockets of their red and black plaid wool shirts and taking them back out again, grinning at one another and at Papa—they had all busted up laughing fit to kill. Uncle R & J Wolf was rolling on the ground, gasping with laughter and saying, "You know it, white man."
>
> It sure did get their goat; they turned without saying a word and walked off toward the highway, red-necked, us laughing behind them. I forget sometimes what laughter can do. (92)

Remembering what laughter can do, Bromden begins to see the comedy of his situation. When McMurphy organizes the fishing expedition, Bromden wants to go, but is afraid to expose his deaf and dumb act.

> I kept getting this notion that I wanted to sign the list. And the more he talked about fishing for Chinook salmon the more I wanted to go. I knew it was a fool thing to want; if I signed up it'd be the same as coming right out and telling everybody I wasn't deaf. If I'd been hearing all this talk about boats and fishing it'd show I'd been hearing everything else that'd been said in confidence around me for the past ten years. And if the Big Nurse found out about that, that I'd heard all the scheming and treachery that had gone on when she didn't think anybody was listening, she'd hunt me down with an electric saw, fix me where she *knew* I was deaf and dumb. Bad as I wanted to go, it still made me smile a little to think about it: I had to keep on acting deaf if I wanted to hear at all. (197)

That night Bromden's comic sense develops further. McMurphy discovers the collection of chewing gum stuck underneath the Chief's bed and begins to sing the comic song, "does the Spearmint lose its flavor on the bedpost o-ver niiiite?" Although the Chief is initially angry with McMurphy for making fun of him, he soon begins to perceive his own comedy.

> But the more I thought about it the funnier it seemed to me. I tried to stop it but I could feel I was about to laugh—not at McMurphy's singing, but at my own self. (205)

The Chief must regain his laugh before he can regain his speech, and his first words to McMurphy when he has stopped laughing are "thank you." Having recovered his comic sense, Bromden recovers his health.

But it is not until the fishing expedition that Bromden fully appreciates the comedy of existence. On the boat, when all of the men collapse together in laughter. Bromden joins their human community, both involved and detached at the same time, in the true spirit of high comedy.

> It started slow and pumped itself full, swelling the men bigger and bigger. I watched, part of them, laughing with them—and somehow not with them. I was off the boat, blown up off the water and skating the wind with those black birds, high above myself, and I could look down and see myself and the rest of the guys, see the boat rocking there in the middle of those diving birds, see McMurphy surrounded by his dozen people, and watch them, us, swinging a laughter that rang out

> on the water in ever-widening circles, farther and farther, until it crashed up on beaches all over the coast, on beaches all over all coasts, in wave after wave after wave. (238)

Participating in the cosmic comedy, Bromden learns that if laughter cannot ultimately defeat death and failure, that fact need not prevent one from acting. At the close, during the orgy, Bromden can even laugh in the very heart of the Combine.

The final result of the Chief's new knowledge is the novel itself. Bromden learns to perceive his life as a comic fiction and to transform that fiction into art. Laughing at himself and his society, he writes a novel that makes the reader laugh, thus perpetuating his own comic vision. Form and content merge as Bromden writes a book in praise of laughter that itself induces laughter.

The very act of writing the novel is a means of fighting the humorous society, ridiculing it through comedy and subtly shifting the reader's vision. Wylie Sypher notes that, like the joke or the dream, "any truly creative work of art [is] a form of 'interruption' of our normal patterns or designs of seeing and speaking."[22] As comic artist, Bromden manages to shift the reader's patterns of vision and expectation. Although the Chief's perceptions at the outset seem comically distorted, they gradually reveal a metaphoric truth. As a comic poet, Bromden translates the unseen into the seen, the abstract into the concrete, giving the Nurse's hatred or the patients' frustrations palpable, visible form. The Nurse thus becomes, metaphorically, a locomotive, Harding's hands are graceful birds; Bancini's fist is a big, rusty iron ball. Even Colonel Matterson's babblings are poetic. "It's true," says the Chief. "I can see what he's driving at. . . . Mexico *is* like a walnut; it's brown and hard and you feel it. . . . You're making sense, old man, a sense of your own" (129). Similarly, if the Nurse does not actually have a plastic face, if Ellis's urine doesn't actually rot the floor beneath his feet, if the attendants are not actually full of cogs and gears, the descriptions provide an accurate picture of the mechanization and hatred rampant in the Chief's world. In the end the Chief himself perceives that his visions are metaphorically, if not literally, true. "But it's the truth even if it didn't happen" (8).

It is finally the Chief, then, and not McMurphy, who embodies the novel's comic values. McMurphy dies; the Chief lives on as a distinct individual, not merely as a reincarnation of Mc-

Murphy as some critics have suggested. The Chief, for example, never adopts McMurphy's attitude toward violence and sex, nor does he reflect the machismo values of his hero. Bromden creates in McMurphy an extremity of total freedom as a balance to the nurse's extremity of total control, in an effort to locate the mean. He renders both characters comic in order to expose the flaws inherent in both approaches to human existence.

Faced with two extreme choices—the sterility, total control, and deadly order of the Combine, or the obsessive sexuality, total freedom, and chaos of McMurphy—the Chief resists both. If Bromden has learned anything from his experience, it's to be himself, to refuse to let others remake him in their image.

> I'd take a look at my own self in the mirror and wonder how it was possible that anybody could manage such an enormous thing as being what he was. There'd be my face in the mirror, dark and hard, with big, high cheekbones like the cheek underneath them had been hacked out with a hatchet, eyes all black and hard and mean-looking just like Papa's eyes or the eyes of all those tough mean-looking Indians you see on TV, and I'd think, That ain't me, that ain't my face. It wasn't even me when I was trying to be that face. I wasn't even really me then; I was just being the way I looked, the way people wanted. It don't seem like I ever have been me. (153)

At the end, Chief Bromden has recreated himself in his own best image: strong, independent, sensitive, sympathetic, and loving, with a comic perspective on his human limitations. As an artist Bromden manages to combine the vitality, spontaneity, and freedom of McMurphy with the control and form of art. Freedom without form results in McMurphy's destruction. Form without freedom results in the horrors of the Combine. Writing a novel that combines both freedom and form, fictionalizing experience to give it meaning, maintaining the proper comic perspective on self and society, Bromden represents Kesey's hope for the future:

> The Good Guys will win. The consciousness now being forged will hang, tempered and true, in the utility closet alongside old and faithful tools like Mercy and Equality and Will Rogers.[23]

It's what laughter can do.

Unlike Todd, Skipper, and even Humbert, Bromden cannot create a new, imaginative world around himself. But armed with love, understanding, and laughter, he can escape the humorous society of the institution and dedicate himself to freedom and life. Things are not so clear cut for J. Henry Waugh, hero and proprietor of Robert Coover's *The Universal Baseball Association.* Like Bromden, Henry seems to escape his humorous society. Like Todd and Skipper, he manages to create an alternative reality. But like Humbert, he is obsessed with his imaginative vision, and his created world may be a mere delusion. By the end of the novel, the baseball association has taken on a life of its own, and Henry has completely disappeared. Combining themes introduced by Barth, Hawkes, Nabokov, and Kesey, Coover examines the very origins of history and belief, exploring the philosophical implications inherent in a comic vision of reality.

VI.

The Great American Game *Robert Coover's* The Universal Baseball Association, Inc. J. Henry Waugh, Prop.

Although Robert Coover's *The Origin of the Brunists* won the William Faulkner Award for the best first novel of 1967, and although his 1969 collection of stories, *Pricksongs & Descants*, won him additional critical recognition as a writer of "metafictions," little serious attention has been paid his important second novel, *The Universal Baseball Association, Inc. J. Henry Waugh, Prop.* Combining a traditional strong narrative story line with a contemporary self-consciousness about technique, the novel is Coover's best, reflecting the same themes and concerns as the better known novels in this study: human creativity, the problem of evil, the role of the artist, the deterioration of modern society, the comedy of history, the origins of belief, the nature of "reality." And, like most contemporary American writers', Coover's work is deeply and profoundly comic. Coover himself notes in an interview:

> I tend to think of tragedy as a kind of adolescent response to the universe—the higher truth is a comic response. . . . There *is* a kind of humor extremity which is even more mature than the tragic response. Now that may seem in fact tragic. Thus some of the great ironic, comic fiction can nevertheless be equal to the same kind of strange emotion you get out of tragedy because your emotions can be mixed.[1]

One of the themes of *The Universal Baseball Association* is the potentially tragic assumption that comedy is a more mature response to the problems of the human condition than is tragedy.

Critics, however, have generally either ignored the book or found it disappointing. One early reviewer, for example, dismissed it as a "mildly amusing satire" that "becomes a smothering bore."[2] More recently, Neil Schmitz has insisted that the novel "collapses upon its hollow absurdist center, fails because Coover does not possess the sinew of Barth's intellect, the embittered but wholly dedicated urgency of his questions."[3] The few critics who have tried to rescue the novel from such judgments have treated it as an allegory. Jackson Cope, for example, argues, among other things, that the novel is a political allegory, reflecting the assassination of Jack Kennedy (Jock Casey) and the turmoil surrounding the Vietnam War. For Cope, Fennimore McCaffree, the Legalist chancellor of the UBA, is Lyndon Johnson, and the Guildsman party, one of the conflicting political factions in the book, is composed of Goldwaterites. The novel thus embodies the "history of the USA in the sixties" with "the surge of revolution rolling in from the future."[4] Max Schulz, on the other hand, describes the novel as a religious allegory. For Schulz, Henry is God, Damon is the "ritual god of nature," Jock Casey is Jesus Christ, Barney Bancroft is "a representative of the Hebrew Sanhedrin," and Patrick Monday is Saint Paul.[5] Although the political and religious references are important for the novel, the one-to-one correspondence suggested by Cope and Schulz breaks down. The novel is not simply an allegory, nor is it primarily a satire, nor does it lack "urgency" or "intellect." *The Universal Baseball Association* is instead an extremely complex comic fiction that uses literary and historical allusion to probe deeply into the central metaphysical questions of the nature of reality and the origins of belief.

One probable reason for the novel's rather pale critical reception and comparative neglect is its subject matter. The focus of Coover's novel is not on the pervasive conflict between the Individual and the Institution, as in *One Flew Over the Cuckoo's Nest* or *Catch-22*, nor on the consequences of war and violence in the modern world, as in *The Floating Opera* and *Second Skin.* Instead, Coover chooses to write about baseball, recalling Ring Lardner's comic and inconsequential tales and Malamud's rather thin comic parable. But Coover's is no ordinary baseball tale, as is evident from even a capsule summary of the plot.

J. Henry Waugh is a lonely bachelor accountant with a fondness for B-girls and beer who has invented numerous games, "baseball, basketball, different card games, war and finance games, horseracing, football, and so on, all on paper of course," to fill up a rather empty existence.[6] Having grown weary of his brilliant "Intermonop," "using twelve, sixteen, or twenty-four boards at once and an unlimited number of players" (44),

Henry has returned to baseball as his "final great project" (19). Modeled on real baseball, which he finds "boring," Henry's game is played with three dice and some complex charts that account for the varying abilities of players in a league he has imaginatively created. In addition to recording the usual statistics on batting, pitching, and scoring, Henry determines births and deaths, inventing personal histories for each player in the league, and, at times, even adopting their personalities.

Now in its fifty-sixth season, the game has become an obsession with its creator, disrupting his efficiency as an accountant in the firm of "Dunkelmann, Zauber & Zifferblatt, Licensed Tax & General Accountants, Specializing in Small Firms, Bookkeeping Services & Systems, Payrolls & Payroll Taxes, Monthly, Quarterly & Annual Audits, Enter Without Knocking" (35), and he's in danger of losing his job. When Damon Rutherford, a young rookie pitcher who has revitalized the game, is killed by a beanball (a roll of 1–1–1 on the dice), both of Henry's worlds fall apart. Neglecting his job, he commits himself even more deeply to the game by manipulating the dice so that Jock Casey, Damon's killer, will be hit fatally by a line drive from catcher Royce Ingram, Damon's battery mate. Henry's interference disrupts the lives of his players, who break up into political factions and religious sects, questioning the very nature of their reality and the game in which they play. At the end, one hundred seasons later, Waugh has disappeared from the book, but the game goes on, the players having turned the two deaths into an annual religious ritual with young rookies assuming the roles of Damon and Jock.

Although the book is about a good deal more than baseball, baseball is central, and is, in some ways, an inspired choice of subject matter for a novel about America, history, myth, religion, art, and imagination. Baseball, as perhaps everyone in America knows, is "The Great American Game" (Henry himself calls it that several times in the novel) and has had an almost religious following. Henry describes his first experience of a real baseball game in terms that reflect the early enthusiasm:

> "I felt like I was part of something there, you know, like in church, except it was more *real* than any church, and I joined in in the score-keeping, the hollering, the eating of hotdogs and drinking of Cokes and beer, and for a while I even had the funny idea that ball stadiums and not European churches were

> the real American holy places." Formulas for energy configurations where city boys came to see their country origins dramatized, some old lost fabric of unity. (166)

The mythic origins of baseball are important for the novel and will be discussed later. Here, Coover may be parodying America's penchant for deifying its sports heroes. But even if we no longer respond to baseball with the kind of awe Henry describes, the game has been absorbed into American culture more deeply than may at first be apparent. Nearly every American has, at one time or another, "had two strikes against him" or been "way off base." Even people who have never seen a game will occasionally "have something on the ball," or "throw someone a curve," or "pinch-hit" or "go to bat" for a friend. We've all had a few "close calls" or "made a hit" with someone or felt that someone was "out of our league." Every American adolescent male has prided himself on getting to first base and beyond with his favorite girl friend. Even recent presidents of the United States have resorted to baseball terminology in describing their political philosophies. Baseball slang has entered our language, subtly modifying our perceptions of "reality."

It is the curious balance between this folk aspect of baseball (linguistic, religious, mythic) and the scientific aspect (statistical, numerical, historical) that stimulates Henry's imagination. As Henry notes, baseball "had struck on an almost perfect balance between offense and defense, and it was that balance, in fact, that and the accountability—the beauty of the records system which found a place to keep forever each least action—that had led Henry to baseball as his final great project" (19). The appeal of baseball is as much statistical as heroic, as much a ritual of numbers and record keeping as of manly encounter and athletic skill. Henry thus bases his players' performance on predetermined numerical probabilities and their life expectancy on insurance actuarial tables.

Although the rules, statistics, records, and probabilities of baseball appeal to Henry, it is the folk aspect of the game that ultimately gives it life. The numbers don't explain everything; they allow for surprises, upsets, and turnabouts as well. The overall design of the game thus accommodates luck, accident, even malevolence, and Henry turns these possibilities into legends and folk songs about his players. Early in the novel, Henry muses on this curious dual aspect of baseball. "No other activity in the world had so precise and comprehensive a history, so specific an ethic, and at the same time, strange as it seemed, so much ultimate mystery" (45).

Henry's game thus incorporates real baseball's balance of scientific record keeping and supernatural mythmaking. But the game reflects real baseball in even more literal ways. As Henry explains, the names of his eight teams are taken from real teams in baseball history, and the inspiration for the plot of the novel may derive from the story of a real player. Lamenting Damon Rutherford's death, Henry tells his friend, Lou, the story of James Creighton. "When Jim Creighton died, the boys crowned his grave with a fantastic monument. It had crossed bats on it and a baseball cap and even a base and up on top a giant baseball. Or maybe it was the world. They probably no longer knew the difference" (89). James Creighton is an historical figure, remembered as the first professional ballplayer. Pitching brilliantly for the Brooklyn Excelsiors in 1862, he sustained "an internal injury occasioned by strain" while batting and died a few days later. The players adorned his grave with the monument Henry describes, and the Excelsiors, like the Pioneers after Damon's death and the Knickerbockers after Jock Casey's, proceeded to lose most of the rest of their games.[7] It is likely that Jim Creighton provided a model for Jock Casey or Damon Rutherford.

Similarly, several of baseball's early rule makers and innovators suggest models for Henry. Alexander J. Cartwright, who proposed the first list of American rules and coached the Knickerbockers in their loss of the first recorded game, 23–1, in 1845 and William Henry Wright, the captain of the first professional team, the Cincinnati Red Stockings, or "Beaneaters," both resemble Henry in more than name. Henry Chadwick, a sportswriter who invented the box score, authored the first rule book, and was affectionately called "The Father of the Game," offers an even more striking resemblance. Since Coover is obviously well versed in baseball history, it is likely that Henry is, in part, a combination of these early figures.[8]

In some ways, then, the novel can be seen as a parody of baseball history, a parody that extends to the very origins of the game. At the turn of the century, as baseball began to gain phenomenal popularity, Albert G. Spalding, the sporting goods baron, wanted to prove the game wholly American, "the exponent of American Courage, Confidence, Combativeness; American Dash, Discipline, Determination; American Energy, Eagerness, Enthusiasm."[9] Consequently Spalding forwarded the myth of the "immaculate conception," in which Abner Doubleday, destined to be a Civil War hero, is supposed to have "invented" the game of baseball one afternoon in 1839. The myth was certified as official in 1907, and thirty years later the baseball world solemnly celebrated the centennial of its "birth."[10] Henry feels somewhat uncomfortable about the origins of his own game. As he notes, "the abrupt beginning had its disadvantages. It was, in a sense, too arbitrary, too inexplicable" (45). Henry, of course, hasn't any more invented his game than Abner Doubleday invented ours. Both are based on games that went before, having evolved over centuries. Coover thus parodies the myth of baseball's origins, the fans' subsequent deification of the players, and the transformation of hot dogs and beer into an American religious communion. The reader who misses the parody of baseball lore and legend misses a subtle element in the humor of the book.

Although Henry's game is thus based on real baseball, the fact that it is not "real" accounts for the most obvious comedy in the book. The discrepancy between the "real" world and Henry's imaginary one provides the incongruity necessary for comedy. The novel opens as a conventional baseball novel might, in the middle of a game. Damon Rutherford, Henry's exciting new rookie pitcher, is just six outs away from pitching a perfect game. The players are tense, the crowd is excited, and Henry, ostensibly sitting in the bleachers, is ecstatic. "More than just another ball game now: *history*!" (3). With the action at its peak, however, Henry takes "the occasion of this seventh-inning hometown stretch to hurry downstairs to the delicatessen to get a couple sandwiches" (4). The basic narrative device used to achieve comic effects early in the novel, then, is the juxtaposition of incongruous worlds. Coover draws the reader into the imaginary game and then casually jolts him back into the "real" world.

As the action continues, the discrepancy between the two worlds widens. While the baseball game takes on almost metaphysical significance, Henry's activity becomes increasingly mundane and physical. " 'Nothing like this before.' Yes, there was a soft murmur pulsing through the stands: nothing like it, electrifying, new, a new thing, happening here and now! Henry paused to urinate" (11). But as the reader's perception of the comic discrepancy grows, Henry's seems to disappear. When Benny Diskin, who works in the delicatessen, brings Henry his sandwich, Henry subsumes him in the game. "Haymaker manager Rag (Pappy) Rooney stroked his lean grizzly jaw, gave the nod to Everts. 'How's that, Mr. Waugh?'" Benny Diskin responds, puzzled by Henry's nod to him (5). The two worlds soon merge even more inextricably in Henry's mind, as the increasingly ambiguous pronoun references show. "Law grinned, nodded at old Maggie, stuffed a chaw of gum into his cheek. In the kitchen, he tore open the six-pack of beer" (6).

Through the course of the novel, Henry's obsession with the game gradually takes over his life, eventually destroying his equilibrium and usurping "reality." From the outset, for example, Henry's friends and acquaintances have their assigned parallels in his baseball league. Pete, of Pete's Bar, is Jake Bradley, a retired ballplayer, and his juke box plays country-and-western songs written by pitcher Sandy Shaw. Henry's best friend, Lou, is a reincarnated Holly Tibbet, reflecting the catcher's love of good food and fear of fast women. Hettie, the B-girl in Jake's (Pete's) Bar, is Knickerbocker manager Sycamore Flynn's virgin daughter, with whom Henry, posing as Damon Rutherford, has a "consecratory romp" after the perfect game (43).

Although Henry has managed to keep the two worlds separate through the first fifty-five seasons, the balancing act has become increasingly difficult. He begins to see cars as dejected players and policemen as coaches waving their runners home (46). He also begins unconsciously to assume the personalities of his players in public places. Sitting at his desk at DZ&Z, for example, musing on Damon Rutherford's perfect game, Henry answers his employer, Mr. Zifferblatt, with Damon's voice, "How's that, fella?" (42). On the night of Damon Rutherford's wake in Jake's Bar, Henry "becomes" several players at once, obviously disrupting the bar and making a fool of himself, alienating both Pete and Hettie. By the end of the novel, Henry, who has increasingly merged with his game, vanishes, perhaps absorbed completely by it.

Thus Henry seems to be in the comic tradition of the deluded protagonist, the self-deceived character whose "fixed idea" or obsession renders him humorous. The "humor" figure has recurred with variations throughout the history of comic literature, from the *alazons* of Aristophanes, through the buffoons of Shakespeare, to the pedants of Fielding and Pope, and this kind of self-deceived protagonist has been a staple of the modern comic novel. Forster's British are obsessed with their own self-importance and hatred of the Indians; Joyce's Stephen is obsessed with his ego and his art; Barth's Todd is obsessed with death, Hawkes's Skipper with his daughter's innocence, and Nabokov's Humbert with his nymphets. J. Henry Waugh is obsessed with his dice game. As in the case of his comic predecessors, Waugh risks being dehumanized by his obsession, and, late in the book, he grows almost demonic, rejecting his few friends.

Hettie Irden is one of the two people with whom Henry tries to share his life. As a B-girl at Pete's Bar, she is no doubt accustomed to peculiar behavior from her clients, and she is happy to play Henry's game. "Hettie had invented her own magic version, stretching out as the field, left hand as first base . . ." (206). Since Henry talks about his players as if they were real, Hettie assumes that they are, and that Henry just enjoys pretending to be those real men. When she discovers that Henry's league is imaginary, that Henry has been pretending to be imaginary characters, she naturally finds the situation humorous. But even her laughter reveals her complete and loving acceptance of Henry:

> She blinked. And then she laughed. Opened her baggy jaws and whooped. "A game!" She looked back at the table, a light dawning. "You mean . . . ? Then that's . . . ! Hey!" She jumped up to paw heedlessly through the papers. "I'll bet old what's his name, Swanee's here, ain't he?" She cackled, rummaging and clawing. "Lookit these names! We can have a orgy, Henry!" Her laughter tore clean through him. She turned on him and tweaked his nose: "Henry, you're a complete nut!" Laughing, grinning, she looked down on him, sighed. "But you're awful sweet, just the same. . . . Anyway, who ain't crazy? I sure ain't got no sense!" (174–75)

At this point, however, Henry has lost all comic perspective of himself and his situation. Obsessed with the game, he cannot laugh with Hettie; he can only reject her. "Ugly and old," he thinks. "She was. They were" (175). Sullenly refusing to give her the expected "benedictive slap on her bottom," thus rejecting *Irden* or "earth," the German meaning of her name, Henry gives up part of his humanity, and Hettie leaves in tears.

Similarly, Henry rejects the man who comes closest to being a real friend, Lou Engel. Throughout the novel, Lou shows concern for Henry, continually inquiring about his well-being, often asking him out for dinner or a movie. Henry usually refuses, insisting that his extra "work" prevents him from coming. Henry feels superior to Lou and scorns him most of the time, but toward the end of the novel, desperate for some human community, he invites Lou over to play the game. While Lou good-naturedly stumbles through the complexities of dice and charts, Henry becomes increasingly impatient with Lou's lack of commitment to the game. When Lou accidentally spills beer on the table, Henry completely rejects him. "*Lou! . . . You clumsy goddamn idiot!* . . . Just get outa the way!" (198–99). Lou silently leaves, whatever slender connection Henry had with ordinary "reality" irrevocably severed.

Henry is, of course, not always self-deceived, and he periodically realizes that his game is dehumanizing him. Midway through the book he perceives his situation with a kind of comic despair:

> And he was old Fennimore McCaffree in his black suit giving orders and Barney Bancroft urging the boys how they had to win this game and all the old Elders sitting like a panel of enraged titans up on the Elders Bench and the catcher Chauncey O'Shea blubbering there behind the plate all broken up by this thing and he was the umpire Frosty Young hollering out they had to play ball no matter what and thinking how hard it was going to be to call them straight though he had to and he was also each of the old-time Pioneers who'd come there for Brock Rutherford Day at Pioneer Park and now a little awe-struck but back there to see this thing out . . . but mostly he was only J. Henry Waugh, pooped and plastered Prop., thinking that this was sure a helluva thing for a grown man to be doing at dawn on a working day. (124–25)

If Henry can, on occasion, see himself in a comic perspective, he can also see the comedy of the world that everyone else in the novel regards as "real." Henry's baseball association may be the product of a diseased imagination, but it also seems to include the beauty, romance, and heroism missing from everyday life. In creating an imaginative world, absurd though it may be, Henry is an artist, and his art satirically exposes the rather unimaginative and dull society in which the other characters play out their lives. Indeed, given a choice between Henry's imaginary baseball world and the "real" world in the novel, the reader would be forced to opt for baseball. If Henry is a comic humor, the real world is composed of a whole series of comic humors fighting for control of the comic society.

Horace Zifferblatt, Henry's boss, is the primary representative of this humorous society. Like Fernandez in *Second Skin*, Zifferblatt wears a snakeskin belt and tyrannizes the protagonist, his name reflecting his comic obsession. In German, *Zifferblatt* means "clock-face," and Henry notes that "the clock on the wall . . . somehow in its fat white roundness and hard black numbers always reminded Henry of Horace Zifferblatt himself" (136). True to his name, Zifferblatt values clock time and efficiency and preaches the Calvinistic doctrine of hard work and reverence for authority on which his world is founded. Since there is no room for "play" in Zifferblatt's world, Henry is forced to describe his baseball game as "work." Lou, for instance, a faithful devotee of Zifferblatt's philosophy, "could accept the idea of taking on outside work for extra money, [but] he'd probably be astonished to learn about the game" (140). Hettie laughs uproariously when she discovers that Henry's "work" is really just a game. Similarly, a "real" death in Ziff's world is an occasion for mourning, but if it's just a part of your imaginative life that dies, no one has the least patience or sympathy.

In some ways, then, the novel is a satire on an atrophied American society that values only work and money and even turns sports into professional activities, into "work." For Henry, this world seems perilously close to constricting the possibilities once and for all. When he walks into a florist's to buy an arrangement for Damon's funeral, Henry discovers that all of the flowers on the walls are plastic. When the florist hands him a wreath and whispers that "it will last forever," Henry is horrified. "But . . . well, that's not the point, is it?" But the florist solemnly intones, "We must keep searching, we must carry on the work, we must resist to the end," envisioning, no doubt, a world encased in plastic for posterity. Henry wonders, "Had they finally found it after all these centuries of search? That Stone of great virtue, called a Stone and not a stone? Next thing, they'd be going off the gold standard, filling Fort Knox with plastics. The quintessence, *huantan*, the sacred stuff" (82). But Henry refuses to accept this picture as the only possible one, and, referring to a newspaper that "spoke blackly of bombs, births, wars, weddings, infiltrations, and social events," he remarks to Lou, "You can take history or leave it, but if you take it you have to accept certain assumptions or ground rules about what's left in and what's left out" (49). Henry realizes what Ziff and Lou and Hettie don't, that there are other possible histories, other possible worlds. Later, when he buys another paper, Henry notes, "Different paper, different headlines, different stories, even different horoscopes. Must be some other world" (142). He sees that Zifferblatt's world, for all its plastic permanence, is just as fictional as Henry's own.

But the novel is not merely a satire on modern society with the artistic imagination as norm. If the "real" world reflects obsessions that rival Henry's own, it also reflects his artistry and provides the human love and compassion (represented by Hettie and Lou) that Henry seems to lack. As is typical of the comic hero, Henry's satiric exposure of his humorous society exposes himself as well.

Ziff's attitude toward his accounting firm, for example, is very much like Henry's toward his game. Henry has charts and records and books on his players; Ziff has his own "diplomas, certificates, photographs, mottos, clippings, charts," and pictures of his deceased partners with the inscription, "*They are with us still*" (138). Further, Ziff uses Henry's baseball metaphor to explain his own philosophy. "A lot of individual stars aren't enough, you've got to have organization and discipline, as well." Finally Ziff tells Henry the story of old Marty Dunkelmann ("gloomy" or "arrogant" in German) who, like Damon Rutherford, died in the line of duty (138–39). The firm of DZ&Z thus stimulates Ziff's imagination as much as the UBA stimulates Henry's. Henry is even forced at one point to agree with Zifferblatt. "Ziff was right: he was getting disorganized. The old menace" (140). Thus the satire here, as in most comedy, goes both ways. Society thinks Henry is crazy, but society's pursuits are much like his. Henry thinks society is crazy, but his pursuits are much like society's.

If Zifferblatt comically doubles Henry's "artistry," Lou is an artist in his own right. As Henry observes with admiration, Lou is a food artist. "It was amazing to watch Lou when he got really attuned to his eating. All clumsiness vanished and his fingers played over the food as upon a musical instrument, his face flushing with pleasure and mild exertion" (133). Later, Lou is an "artist in confrontation with the raw stuff of his vocation" (157). Further, like Lou, Mitch Porter and his waitress are artists. "Mitch Porter knew he was good. Poise: no really great star was ever without it" (154). His waitress, Henry notes, has a "style all her own" (160). Thus, while Henry satirically exposes his society, it exposes him, reflecting both his artistry and his obsession.

What the comic exposure of both Henry and his society finally reveals is the universal need for some order, some meaning, some pattern, to be imposed on the chaos of experience. Zifferblatt finds meaning in Calvinistic virtue; Henry in the complexities of baseball. Both are comic reflectors of a basic human need, and both, curiously enough, owe their origins to religion. Finally, what man seems to require, Coover suggests, is some metaphysical or religious justification of his existence. While this need is certainly comic, even ridiculous, it is nonetheless "real."

As I noted earlier, Henry has no more "invented" his game than Abner Doubleday "invented" modern baseball. Henry's game is merely a variation on real baseball, and real baseball is merely a variation on earlier games. The evolution of baseball has, in fact, been traced to ancient Egyptian religious and fertility rites. As *The Official Encyclopedia of Baseball* explains, baseball seems to be

> derived from religious rites of ancient times, with the fertility (of crops or people) as the main theme. . . . Egyptian king-gods and high priests used a ball as the central symbol of Springtime ceremonies. Authorities disagree as to whether the ball represented the sun (which is the source of life) or the mummified head of Osiris (symbol of growth and fertility). But in either case it is an object of potency. . . . Noticing how tremendously popular were the pagan fertility rites, the Christian church decided to adopt it in their Easter ceremony . . . and records show that early in the 12th century, in the high church of Vienna, the Archbishop would pass a ball back and forth with clerics lined up for the processional. After the services, the Archbishop threw the ball among the assembled people, who followed the Moorish custom of splitting into teams. The popular custom spread throughout France and Spain. Even the cathedral of Rheims wound up Easter services with a ball game.[11]

Modern baseball could thus be seen as a parody of ancient fertility and religious rites. Henry's game, parodying real baseball, comically reveals the mythic residue of the sexual and the spiritual embedded in the Great American Game.

At first, sex in the book seems little more than an occasion for an old joke. Coover notes that Hettie and Henry "often used baseball idiom" (22), and then he multiplies that idiom comically, making use of all the predictable gags about "getting a hit" and "scoring." Early in the book, in celebration of Damon Rutherford's perfect game, Henry adopts Damon's personality to enable him to have sex with Hettie, and the whole encounter turns into a ball game. On the way up to Henry's apartment, Hettie reaches inside his pocket and squeezes his "bat;" when they arrive, play begins:

> "Damon," she whispered, unbuckling his pants, pulling his shirt out. And "Damon," she sighed, stroking his back, unzipping his fly, sending his pants earthward with a rattle of buckles and coins. And "Damon!" she greeted, grabbing—and that girl, with one swing, he knew then, could bang a pitch clean out of the park. "*Play ball!*" cried the umpire. And the catcher, stripped of mask, and guard, revealed as the pitcher Damon Rutherford, whipped the uniform off the first lady ballplayer in Association history, and then, helping and hindering all at once, pushing and pulling, they ran the bases, pounded into first, slid into second heels high, somersaulted over third, shot home standing up, then into the box once more, swing away, and run them all again, and "Damon!" she cried, and "Damon!" (29)

Later Coover uses the baseball metaphor to poke a little fun at Freud. "Mom in a protected crouch, holding up her big padded womb, Dad delivering the pitch, winging it in there, time after time. Looked easy. But she forgot about the batter, not to mention his brothers. Standing there in the box. Frustrating old Dad by poking his own stick out there in the way" (33–34). The ballad of "Long Lew and Fanny" further extends the outrageous sexual humor, the two comic names appropriately describing the anatomical focus of the song. Like Mel Brooks, Coover takes a tired old joke and makes it, improbably, work. By using a cliché with impunity, Coover breaks the rule about using clichés, which is surprising, and therefore funny.

But it soon becomes apparent that Coover's fusion of baseball and sex is more than a mere narrative joke. For Henry and his ballplayers, sex is one possible response to death. Death is a felt presence throughout the novel, from the baseball jargon that uses death as a metaphor for striking out or failing in some way to the charts that provide for the players' actual deaths. In addition to the "Extraordinary Occurrences" chart, by which both Damon Rutherford and Jock Casey die, Henry has another set of charts "for determining who, each year, must die" from more natural causes (20). The players are all aware of their own mortality. "Age. It got them all. . . . All of it worked into the charts. It was something the players had to live with" (167).

And yet sex, as a symbol of union and continuity, seems a possible counter to extinction. When Henry tells Hettie about the players' deaths, it "seemed to excite her," and she squeezes harder on his bat "as though afraid now to let go" (28). Henry's response to Damon's death is to have a determined sexual romp. "Feeling good and mean. Earthy. Crude, in fact. . . . In and out, high and low. Just rear back and burn it in" (170). Similarly, Damon's brother, Brock Rutherford, Jr., "had bolted for home the minute the burial was over, dragging his missus behind him, and there, pressed by an inexplicable urgency, had heisted her black skirts, and without even taking time to drop his pants, had shot her full of seed: yes, caught it! she said, and even he felt that germ strike home" (93). What Hettie Irden ("earth") can do for the players is make them all "forget for a moment that they were dying men" (27). Indeed, at the end of the novel, one hundred seasons in the future, most of the earlier players have sons in the game, carrying on the comic continuity, countering death.

Baseball is thus linked with sex, and both baseball and sex are further linked with religion. Henry thinks of his first night with Hettie, for example, as a "consecratory romp" (43), and the next morning he performs the ritual "ablutions and purifications" (36). But the references to religion are even more specific. Throughout the novel, Coover parodies elements of the Old and New testaments, as well as the more current theological debates about such topics as Foreknowledge, Will, Fate, Predestination, and the notion that God is dead.

For example, Henry's full name, J. Henry Waugh, obviously provides an acronym for *JHWH* or "Yahweh," the Hebrew name for God, and Henry is a comic version of the Judeo-Christian deity, the "proprietor" or "prop" of the modern world. Like God, Henry has created the world of his game; it is he who assigns names and meaning to the players. "Name a man and you make him what he is. . . . The basic stuff is already there. In the name. Or rather: in the naming" (48). Henry makes the rules by which he and his players must abide. "He'd set his own rules, his own limits, and though he could change them whenever he wished, nevertheless he and his players were committed to the turns of the mindless and unpredictable—one might even say, irresponsible—dice. That was how it was" (40). Henry is, of course, not quite so helpless, for he knows a great deal more than his players, and he can interfere with the dice.

For one thing, Henry, like God, is on a different time scheme from his players. He can play a whole season in a few weeks. Also, he knows about his charts; players aren't aware of them. Although Henry thus knows everything about his players and the origin of the rules of their game, they know nothing about him; they can only speculate on his existence. Further, like God, Henry can break the rules. If he is at times an indifferent deity, merely throwing the dice and recording the results, he is at other times a loving or a vengeful god. When the dice decree that Damon Rutherford must die, for example, Henry retaliates by arranging the dice so that they will call for the death of Jock Casey, Damon's murderer. Even when Henry doesn't interfere directly, he seems to exert some mystical influence over the game. "Of course, he hadn't interfered directly in any way, and yet the Pioneers must have felt, somehow, his resistance, and in ways not really visible, he had probably in fact made it harder for them" (60).

Finally, Henry has written a forty-volume history of his Association, a history that resembles the Old Testament in length, technique, and content:

> Into the Book went the whole UBA, everything from statistics to journalistic dispatches, from seasonal analyses to general baseball theory. Everything, in short, worth keeping. Style varied from the extreme economy of factual data to the overblown idiom of the sportswriter, from the scientific objectivity of the theoreticians to the literary speculations of essayists and anecdotalists. There were tape-recorded dialogues, player contributions, election coverage, obituaries, satires, prophecies, scandals. It provided a kind of league's-eye view, since functional details of the game were never mentioned—team analyses, for example, never referred to Stars and Aces except metaphorically, and, intentionally, erred slightly. His own shifting moods, often affected by events in the league, also colored the reports, oscillating between notions of grandeur

> and irony, exultation and despair, enthusiasm and indifference, amusement and weariness. Lately, he had noticed a tendency toward melancholy and sentimentality. (55–56)

If Henry is a comic parody of the Judeo-Christian God, Damon Rutherford is a parody of his son, Jesus Christ. The initial description of Damon suggests the parallel. Damon has "a meditative calm, a gentle brooding concern. . . . self-assurance ennobled with a sense of . . . what? Responsibility maybe. Accountability. . . . Damon a self-enclosed yet participating mystery" (9). A sportswriter characterizes Damon with the appropriately biblical phrase, "He knows" (32). Henry is troubled by his growing emotional commitment to Damon, who "meant more to him than any player should" (38). But when Hettie asks him who Damon Rutherford is, Henry replies, "Me," and for a night in bed, he is (26). Finally, Lou thinks that Damon is Henry's bastard son, which, in a comic sense, is what Christ was to God (89). Thus, just as Christ is both son of man and son of God, and God himself, so Damon is son of Brock, son of Henry, and Henry himself. Participating in this trinity, Damon is killed by a number on the dice symbolic of the three in one, 1–1–1.

After Damon's death, as after Adela's "rape" in *A Passage to India*, the world goes insane. The apocalypse prophesied in the book of Revelation seems at hand as evil is loosed from the darkness, order breaks down, and chaos is rampant. Jock Casey, "a hard-bitten cold-blooded sonuvabitch" (128) and the agent of Rutherford's death, thus becomes Antichrist, or perhaps Judas or Caesar, the evil force of destruction. While Damon had brought light and hope to a deteriorating game, "Casey had put out the light and everybody was playing in the dark" (136). The number on the dice that kills Casey is 666, the number of the beast in Revelation. Also, after killing Damon with a beanball, Casey, like the beast, leaves his mark on the right hand of another player, McDermott, by breaking his finger. Only by killing Casey can Henry restore balance and order to his game.

Lou Engel's role in the allegory suggests Satan's. His name translates from German as "angel," and he behaves at times much like Lucifer, the fallen angel. When he joins Henry in his game, for example, Lou brings a red-hot pizza, and, with no heed to the rules, begins making replacements and substitutions, wiping his greasy fingers on the charts, nearly destroying everything with a "flood" of beer. Finally Henry has to banish Lou. "*You clumsy goddamn idiot*!" he shouts (199).

Thus the novel is in some ways a comic allegory of the Christian myth, poking fun at the attempt to impose sacramental order on the universe. But the novel is obviously more than a simple allegory; while the parallels are obvious and significant, the equations ultimately break down. For example, Jock Casey resembles Christ as well as Antichrist.[12] The initials are identical, and Jock possesses some Christlike qualities that Henry comes to appreciate. "Patient. Yes, give him credit, he was. Enduring. And you had to admit: Casey played the game, heart and soul. Played it like nobody had ever played it before. He circled round the man, viewing him from all angles. Lean, serious, melancholy even. And alone. Yes, above all: alone. . . . Sometimes Casey glanced up at him—only a glance, split-second, pain, a pleading" (201–2). Like Christ, Jock must die to save the world of the game.

Thus Coover refuses to turn the novel into a simple allegory. Parodying Christianity, he, like the players at the end, rejects "the simplistic and pious view of Damon as Good and Jock as Evil" (221). Even Henry, in the guise of Barney Bancroft, eventually decides that the situation is more ambiguous and complex, more shifting and accretive. Planning to write a book entitled *The UBA in the Balance*, "Barney Bancroft had discovered that perfection wasn't a thing, a closed moment, a static fact, but *process*, yes, and the process was transformation, and so Casey had participated in the perfection, too" (212). What Coover is able to do in the end is hold the contradictory possibilities in balance.

Although Henry cannot maintain a sense of balance and proportion between his game and the real world, he is able, finally, to preserve a balance of possibilities within the game itself. What ultimately distinguishes Henry from the other characters in the book, as I have noted, is his ability to project himself imaginatively into other possible lives, examining and even espousing totally antithetical attitudes, and thereby refusing to accept any single view as "the truth." Zifferblatt, Lou, and Hettie all lack this ability, accepting their given "reality" as the only possible one. Since Henry *is* all of his players, he can embody opposing arguments and philosophies. At Damon Rutherford's wake, for example, Henry is Rag Rooney, the cynic and nihilist who sneers, "Bathe 'em in blood, boys! Give 'em the truth! And the truth?

It was raunchy and morbid and arid, but it was all there was" (110), and he is also Barney Bancroft, the philosophical humanist who insists, "The Rutherford spirit . . . will carry the day!" (111). "If Rooney did have the truth, Barney didn't want it" (100). Finally, Henry opts for possibility. "The circuit wasn't closed, his or any other: there were patterns, but they were shifting and ambiguous and you had a lot of room inside them. . . . The game on his table was not a message, but an event: the only signs he had were his own reactions" (143).

The final chapter of the novel summarizes and extends the concerns of the whole book. One hundred seasons later the game has reverted to baseball's origins in religious and fertility rites. The players, now broken up in various sects and schisms, reenact the drama of Damon's and Jock's deaths, while a screaming crowd tries to devour the man playing Damon's role, in a violent communion, and little girls clutch at his crotch (229). Henry's whereabouts are unknown: he may still be throwing the dice somewhere overhead; he may be dead, assassinated with Barney Bancroft, the last player with whom he had identified; he may be living in some adjacent world, having abandoned the game to its own devices; he may even have been absorbed into the game itself, since one of the young players, Raspberry Schultz, is a "gentle folklorist and gamesplayer" (231) who "plays himself some device with dice" (234). The chapter is structured on three general responses to the situation: the skeptical questionings of Hardy Ingram-Damon Rutherford, the cynical and humorous negations of Cuss McCamish and several other minor players, and the final conversion and acceptance of Paul Trench-Royce Ingram.

Hardy Ingram, selected to play Damon in the Parable of the Duel, is decidedly ambivalent. Since he is the best rookie, he feels that he should be playing the role, but at the same time he doesn't really believe in it. Neither he nor the reader ever knows for sure whether the ritual will result in his actual death, but he naturally resents the possibility that it may. Ingram has carefully examined the conflicting interpretations various players have imposed on history, and he remains skeptical:

> Book he's been reading lately. *The Doubter.* One of the flood of centennial Bancroft biographies out this year. Author tries to show that Barney Bancroft, not Rutherford or Casey or Hardy's own progenitor Royce Ingram, was actually the central figure,

> the real heart and point of the Parable of the Duel, as they call it now. Rutherford and Casey seem to be giants, this guy claims, but are really only subhuman masks, predesigned roles, while Bancroft is the only one wholly rounded and thus truly human participant in that incredible drama. Maybe the only *real* one. . . . Other theories have Brock Rutherford, Sycamore Flynn, Fennimore McCaffree, Chauncey O'Shea, even Flynn's or McCaffree's daughters at the center. Can't even be sure about the simple *facts*. Some writers even argue that Rutherford and Casey never existed—nothing more than another of the ancient myths of the sun, symbolized as a victim slaughtered by the monster or force of darkness. History: in the end, you can never prove a thing. (223–24)

Although he can't respond wholeheartedly to the situation, he is committed to it and vows "to take it like a man. Like *the* man himself. Poised. Knowing. Cool" (220). He scoffs at the numerology, that "Damon was killed in Game 49: seven times seven," a "fact" that the reader knows to be false. But he finds both Damon and Jock compelling, and when Cuss McCamish and Skeeter Parsons advise him to duck or to refuse to participate, temptations paralleling Christ's, Ingram resists them. A skeptic and a rationalist, Ingram rejects the "simple-minded faith in the ultimate power of justice and truth" but nevertheless recognizes the need for such imaginative constructs. Coover explains, "Invention . . . implies a need and need implies purpose; accident implies nothing, nothing at all, and nothing is the one thing that scares Hardy Ingram" (224–25).

Cuss McCamish is decidedly less ambivalent. A cynic and a nihilist, he completely rejects the ritual, ridiculing it. "*Hang down you heads, old pricks, and pee, it's the boy with the matchstick arm!*" he sings, parodying Sandy Shaw's threnody (225). McCamish, "negator even of negations" (230), sees the sun as a hundred-watt bulb, calls God a "nut," and insists that the players are "mere ideas, hatched whole and hapless, here to enact old rituals of resistance and rot" for the whore, Dame Society (230). Although from the reader's viewpoint this position seems fairly close to the truth, Coover's omniscient voice seems to undercut it. Coover describes McCamish and his friends as "reluctant participants in a classic plot, too wise to fable a future fortune, too distressed ever to invent their childhoods, left with nothing but the spikey imprint of their cleats upon the turf and the passage from envelope to maddening envelope of inscrutable space" (230). Despite their rejection of the ritual, McCamish and his friends are inextricably caught up in it. The young players' very names begin to metamorphosize into those of their counterparts in the ritual. Costen McCamish, playing Tuck Wilson, becomes Cusstuck McWilson. Squire Flint, playing Drew McDermott, becomes Squire McFlint and then Drusquire McWormy. Raspberry Schultz, playing Witness York, becomes Witberry Yultz and then Witless Jerkberry. Skeeter Parsons, playing Toby Ramsey, becomes Parson Ramsey and then Skeetoby Ramparts. McCamish's negations cannot compete with the human need for mystery and meaning.

Paul Trench's response to the ritual is neither the skeptical ambivalence of Hardy Ingram nor the cynical negation of Cuss McCamish. Trench's response is pure dread and fear. As a kind of existential figure facing an abyss of meaninglessness, "at the grim edge, too wise to step back and too frightened to leap," Trench is "afraid. Not only of what he must do. But of everything. Beyond each game, he sees another, and yet another, in endless and hopeless succession. . . . What difference, in the terror of eternity, does it make?" (238). Trench has read all the books interpreting his world's history; he has carefully and agonizingly considered all the possibilities, from McCamish's negations to his father's claims of "sacred duty" (239). Although the other players label him a Damonite, Trench "knows he is nothing" (239). At one point he even considers rebelling against the whole thing and "quitting" or "striking out," refusing to hit the ritual beanball in atonement for Damon's death (241). But Trench cannot accept McCamish's cynicism, which "cuts him off from any sense of wonder or mystery, makes life nothing more than getting by with the least pain possible." For Paul Trench, "such a life seems less than human" (240). At the close, Trench's optimism is renewed, his confidence restored, his place in his world assured. Just as Damon had renewed Henry's life earlier in the book, Hardy Ingram now "lights up the whole goddamn world" for Trench, returning the game to the realm of myth:

> "It's not a trial," says Damon, glove tucked in his armpit, hands working the new ball. . . . "It's not even a lesson. It's just what it is." Damon holds up the baseball between them. It is hard and white and alive in the sun. (242)

The discrepancy between the various players' interpretations of their origin and the reader's knowledge of it is comic. While the players speculate on the meaning of their lives and their history, the reader knows that they are merely figments of a lonely bachelor's imagination. But this knowledge comically turns back on the reader, throwing into doubt his own ultimate reality. Henry's game is a copy of a game that is in some ways a copy of certain ancient rites of spring. The players at the end of the novel have instituted a ritual that is a copy of Henry's copy of a copy of an original ritual that may, of course, itself be a copy of something that went before, or may be the work of some cosmic gamesplayer. The parodic multiplication of copies casts doubt on our own reality and meaning, on our own origins and history, on our own notions of a rational, meaningful cosmos. Thus the novel is ultimately a parodic account of how man imposes continuity and order on chaos, inventing his history and his truth to suit his needs.

There are two possible and antithetical interpretations of this situation. For Cuss McCamish, man is tragically trapped in a static world he never made, saddled with a meaningless religion and a dead God, bereft of hope and belief. For Paul Trench, life is comically renewable in a fluid world full of possibility where meaning, arbitrary though it may be, can be imaginatively imposed upon chaos and emptiness. Coover's preferences are clear. In *Pricksongs & Descants*, in a prologue dedicated to Cervantes, Coover articulates a theory of fiction, and of life, that well applies to each of the comic novels discussed in this study:

> We seem to have moved from an open-ended, anthropocentric, humanistic, naturalistic, even—to the extent that man may be thought of as making his own universe—optimistic starting point, to one that is closed, cosmic, eternal, supernatural (in its soberest sense), and pessimistic. The return to Being has returned us to Design, to microcosmic images of the macrocosm, to the creation of Beauty within the confines of cosmic or human necessity, to the use of the fabulous to probe beyond the phenomenological, beyond appearances, beyond randomly perceived events, beyond mere history. But these probes are above all—like your Knight's sallies—challenges to the assumptions of a dying age, exemplary adventures of the Poetic Imagination, high-minded journeys toward the New World and never mind that the nag's a pile of bones.[13]

VII.

No More Happy Endings

In *Cabot Wright Begins*, Doyley Pepscout, a reviewer who is asked to preview Bernie Gladhart's novel about Cabot Wright, concludes:

> The author of this work, at best only mildly entertaining, has continued the growing threat of degeneracy and unhappy endings in fiction. There is not the least question of a doubt in my mind that rape can and perhaps should be treated in literature. But it cannot be treated as Mr. Bernie Gladhart has done in *Indelible Smudge*. Nowhere has he shown the relationship of the youthful rapist to happy older people whom we meet every day in offices and homes, and to a happy America. We are fed only on deviation and mordant thoughts without any higher note. The ending is even less edifying than the bulk of the book. I regret to say that this sordid, often obscure book, without visible motive or meaning, is dispiriting, disquieting, sordid, and utterly without reader-appeal. It is, however, well written and uses an extensive vocabulary.[1]

In some ways Doyley Pepscout's article is a comic exaggeration of current critical attitudes about black humor. Although the reader of *Cabot Wright Begins* knows, from excerpts provided in the text, that Gladhart's novel is quite funny, itself a comic fiction, Pepscout finds nothing at all funny in it. Instead, he focuses his comments on the "blackness" of the book, its "mordant thoughts" and "disquieting" nature. Similarly, many critics of recent fiction have emphasized the blackness over the humor, concluding that the novels are actually more tragic than comic, and more negative than affirmative.

While critics have thus viewed the contemporary American novel as a new phenomenon (black humor) existing outside conventional literary traditions and as an essentially pessimistic or even tragic form, I have argued that recent fiction is squarely in a recognizable comic tradition. Combining satire, irony, wit, humor, and parody, the recent novel employs the conventional character types, plot patterns, and stylistic devices of earlier comedy, while sharing, to some extent, the affirmation typical of the form.

Like earlier comic literature, the contemporary American comic novel makes use of two conventional character types, the *eiron* and the *alazon*, and two corresponding plot patterns, integration and exposure. The *eiron* is the witty self-deprecator, predestined to be an artist, who exposes the more narrow *alazon*. The *alazon* is the boastful antagonist, the impostor or fool who pretends to be more than he is. In earlier comedy the *eiron* and *alazon* were usually separate characters. In Jane Austen's *Emma*, for example, Knightley conflicts with Emma, finally converting her to the social norm, and in Henry James's *The Europeans* Felix Young conflicts with Eugenia, finally expelling her from the society.

Although the major characters in contemporary fiction are rarely pure *eirons* or *alazons*, the minor characters often reflect the pure types. Orr, Yossarian's mentor in Heller's *Catch-22*, who puts crab apples in his cheeks to appear innocent and pretends to be stupid, all the while practicing his crash landings in preparation for his escape, is a clear example of the *eiron*. In an interview, Heller explains, "Orr is the most intelligent person in the book. . . . Orr is playing a game. He is advancing a false self so that even Yossarian feels sorry for him. And all the book long Orr has figured out his survival, and he knows that part of surviving is to conceal his real intentions. . . . In order to keep them secret, he lets himself be considered a dopey kid."[2] Orr, the *eiron*, teaches Yossarian a method of survival. Pretending to know nothing, Orr knows everything.

As Orr is an example of the pure *eiron* in contemporary fiction, the various villains of the novels are pure *alazons*. Heller's General Scheisskopf, Kesey's Big Nurse, Hawkes's Tremlow, Nabokov's Clare Quilty, Coover's Horace Zifferblatt, Vonnegut's Norman Mushari, Friedman's kike man, Baker's Dr. "Messy" Massey, Elkin's Warden Fisher, all share the destructive potential of the *alazon*, a potential that threatened the harmonious society of earlier fiction. In earlier comedy the *alazon* character had to be converted or expelled in order for the fictional society to triumph. In contemporary fiction, since the villain is usually the representative of the society, the best the protagonist can expect to do is to diminish him through laughter or to escape from him. By casting the villain in a comic role, the contemporary novelist undercuts him. Thus, despite the *alazon*'s power, the protagonist usually manages to escape him at least temporarily at the end.

But the conflict of *eiron* and *alazon* is rarely as simple in recent fiction as it was in earlier comedy. One major difference between the recent comic novel and traditional comedy is that whereas the two types were ordinarily kept separate in earlier comedy, they are now usually combined in a single character. This combination accounts for the ambivalent response of many readers to the protagonists.

If most of the protagonists in recent fiction represent a curious combination of the two archetypes, the *alazon* characteristics are perhaps the more obvious. McMurphy and Elliott Baker's Shillitoe, for example, praise "fighting and fucking"; Humbert violates a child and justifies it as beautiful; Roth's Portnoy is ruled by his perpetual erection; Friedman's Stern bounces a woman up on a stick thrust between her legs; Donleavy's Dangerfield puts a pillow over a baby's face; Elkin's Feldman sells his father's body to a hospital and haggles over the price. Such attitudes toward women, children, and parents are characteristic of the *alazon*. It is difficult to affirm a hero who seems so reprehensible so much of the time.

But if the protagonists resemble the *alazon*, becoming the butt of the author's satiric exposure, they also resemble the *eiron*, sharing his self-deprecation and artistry. Todd Andrews constantly undercuts himself, pretending to know nothing about novel writing while crafting a complex, sophisticated fiction and rewriting his own life. Portnoy, for all his problems, knows the value of self-mockery, for "self-depreciation is, after all, a classic form of Jewish humor."[3] McMurphy discovers the usefulness of pretended ignorance and uses his knowledge to defeat Big Nurse. Yossarian learns the *eiron*'s method of survival from Orr and sails off to a mythical Sweden. Pretending to be less than they are, the protagonists learn to be more.

While not all of the protagonists learn the art of innocence, nearly all of them share the *eiron*'s potential artistry. In four of the five novels I have discussed at length, the protagonists themselves write the works they're in: Todd Andrews, Skipper, Humbert Humbert, and Chief Bromden all re-create their own lives as works of fiction. Many of the other heroes of contemporary comic fiction are writers as well: Portnoy is a playwright and prose poet; Dangerfield, Jong's Isadora Wing, and Shillitoe are poets; Purdy's Gladhart is a novelist; Vonnegut's Rosewater is a poet and novelist; Rita Mae Brown's Mollie Bolt is a filmmaker. The profession of artist has clear symbolic implications. X. O. Waterfall, the poet and critic in Baker's *A Fine Madness*, explains: "Mr. Shillitoe seems determined to stand apart and forge a new poetry. And, since poetry cannot be divorced from the warp and woof of all life, he has taken on himself the task of formulating a new philosophy, a new religion, a new politics, a new version of history and even at times a new language."[4] John Hawkes echoes Waterfall when he agrees that the contemporary writer has the "absolute need to create from the imagination a totally new and necessary fictional landscape or visionary world."[5] The artist-heroes, like the novelists themselves, seem determined to use their art to create a new vision of the self and the world.

Even when the protagonist is not literally an artist, he characteristically responds to experience with an artist's eye, in an effort to celebrate life and creation in the face of death and destruction. Cabot Wright, for example, frames his life as a work of art so that he can know himself and his perversity and thereby go on to become someone different; Eliot Rosewater affirms that he is "going to be an artist. . . . I'm going to love these discarded Americans, even though they're useless and unattractive. *That* is going to be my work of art."[6] Even Nabokov's humorous Kinbote concludes, "I may assume other disguises, other forms, but I shall try to exist. . . . sans anything but . . . art."[7] Sharing both the *alazon*'s destructiveness and the *eiron*'s creativity, the contemporary comic hero is thus a combination of types, a combination that elicits from the reader contradictory responses. While the reader must reject the protagonist's insensitivity and ignorance, he must embrace his self-deprecation and artistry. The trick is to keep the ambivalent responses in balance.

Two basic plot patterns traditionally correspond to the two character types. The first pattern traces the integration of a character into society, an integration that often takes the form of marriage or surrogate marriage. Shakespeare's romance comedies reflect this pattern. The second pattern consists of a movement that makes all the actions of a character work against him. Meredith's theory of comedy as the moral scourge of stupidity and egotism reflects this pattern.

In recent fiction the exposure plot is most evident, tracing the conscious and unconscious exposure of the protagonist. But whereas in earlier comedy society or its representative exposed an aberrant character in an effort to convert or expel him, now the aberrant character exposes the society in an effort to defeat or escape it. Established society in the contemporary novel is usually satirically exposed as destructive, mechanistic, and sick, a world in which human values have been inverted. Thus in *One Flew Over the Cuckoo's Nest* and *A Fine Madness* the doctors are sicker than the patients; in *Catch-22* the generals are less competent than the privates; in Elkin's *A Bad Man* the guards are more criminal than the inmates; in *Rubyfruit Jungle* heterosexuals are more perverse than homosexuals. With this reversal of traditional expectations, the "bad man" becomes good, the sick person healthy, the amoral moral, the unheroic heroic. Although this situation is more prevalent in contemporary comedy, it has obvious precedents in earlier fiction. The same kind of reversal structures *Great Expectations*, *A Portrait of the Artist*, and *Huckleberry Finn*. As in those earlier comic fictions, the contemporary hero is rarely content merely to expose his humorous society. Instead, he exerts a great deal of energy in an effort to escape the old society by imagining a new one in its place.

If, with some exceptions, the typical ending of earlier comedy focused integration and conversion, the typical ending of contemporary comedy focuses exposure and escape. It is to these endings that most critics look when arguing that the novels are nihilistic or pessimistic fables of despair. When Conrad Knickerbocker insists that "there are no more happy endings,"[8] he refers to the fact that contemporary fiction rarely ends with marriage or with the integration of a character into established society. That conventional kind of "happiness" is not available to characters in novels like *Lolita*, *Catch-22*, and *One Flew Over the Cuckoo's Nest*. Yet, if traditional definitions of "happiness" often don't apply, most of the novels do boast affirmative endings; in some cases, there could be no *more happy* ending. Skipper creates a pastoral island based on love and compassion and fathers a son. Shillitoe finds a safe place with Rhoda in Cob City, Indiana, where "for the first time in his life he was completely independent with poetry his only care." Although he has been lobotomized, he finishes his poem (he had "never been able to confine an idea to his brain"), and he leaves behind him a renewed Dr. Wren, who vows never to let Massey operate again.[9] Stern, having experienced a ritual death and embraced a half-man and a cleaning lady, confronts his enemy, the kike man, and closes the novel in a loving embrace with his wife and child. Rosewater, after suffering a lifetime of misunderstanding and hostility at the hands of society, defeats his enemies and embraces life by adopting fifty-seven fatherless children as his own. Waugh fathers a world more to his liking and disappears into it. Mollie Bolt, caught in a Humbertian world of perversion and sexual confusion, resolves to make something of it, concluding that "one way or another I'll make those movies and I don't feel like having to fight until I'm fifty. But if it does take that long then watch out world because I'm going to be the hottest fifty-year-old this side of the Mississippi."[10] Even when the heroes can only flee, they usually flee *to* something, if only to an imaginary ideal place. That Yossarian will never be able to sail to Sweden, that Bromden may never actually see Canada, is not ultimately important. Yossarian's Sweden, Bromden's Canada, and Pynchon's Vheissu are not so much "real" places where the heroes can be expected to arrive as they are metaphors for human possibility. If the characteristic plot pattern of earlier comedy traced the integration into a preexistent society, often through marriage, the typical plot of the contemporary comic novel reveals escape, often through the creation of an imaginative world around the central character, a world that may be delusive, obsessive, and tenuous but that nevertheless affirms survival and comic continuity.

It is perhaps a mistake, however, to argue from the endings. As L. J. Potts emphasizes, "it is not the happy ending that makes a comedy."[11] Certain types of plot and character determine the comic form, and not any criterion of "happiness." When Prospero and Miranda return to the very society that originally exiled them, we cannot conclude that the ending is "happy." When Dionysus of Aristophanes' *The Frogs* returns with Aeschylus from Hades to the rapidly decaying Athenian society that will reject him, we can but painfully smile. When Mirabel marries Millamant and prepares to live in a chattering, hypocritical society, we perceive that the end is likewise far from "happy." The greatest comedies, as evidenced by Shakespeare, Aristophanes, and Congreve, characteristically reveal sobering endings.

The lack of a conventionally happy ending does not, moreover, prevent these novels from being ultimately affirmative. Throughout the novels, faced with violence, absurdity, and destruction, the contemporary novelists and their protagonists insist on the necessity of life, creation, and a comic perspective on the self and society. Robert Scholes sums it up well:

> What man must learn is neither scorn nor resignation, . . . but how to take a joke. . . . The best response is neither acquiescence nor bitterness. It is first of all a matter of perception. One must "get" the joke. Then one must demonstrate this awareness by playing one's role in the joke in such a way as to turn the humor back on the joker or cause it to diffuse itself harmlessly on the whole group which has participated in the process of the joke.[12]

Thus Todd Andrews adopts the role of comic spirit and rewrites his life; Skipper refuses to fight violence with violence and instead embraces the humorousness of his innocence; McMurphy restores life to the inmates of the asylum by teaching them how to laugh; Cabot Wright recovers from his sexual obsessions by finally laughing at himself and his situation; Waugh and Humbert laugh at the absurdity around them and create worlds more to their liking; Stern faces his ulcer, symbol of his various comic inadequacies, and affirms "if necessary, by God, he would live with the damned thing;"[13] Feldman, in his blue fool suit, communicates with the other prisoners through laughter and finally arrives at a vision of his own innocence.

If the protagonist of the contemporary American comic novel doesn't always "get the joke," the novelist and the reader do. The affirmation for the reader who gets the joke is an affirmation of the individual over society, energy over passivity, imagination over convention, freedom over control, love over hate, life over death. The world may be grotesque, violent, and destructive. Possibilities for happiness may seem slim indeed. But, with Portnoy, the reader learns to "pluck laughter from despair."[14] With Cabot Wright the reader affirms, "We was here, finally laughed."[15]

End Notes

Notes to Chapter I.

1. Melvin Maddocks, "We Are Not Amused—And Why," p. 31.
2. Wylie Sypher, "The Meanings of Comedy," in *Comedy*, ed. Wylie Sypher, pp. 195, 196, 201.
3. James Purdy, *Cabot Wright Begins* (New York: Farrar, Straus & Giroux, 1964), p. 210.
4. Louis D. Rubin, Jr., ed., *The Comic Imagination in American Literature*, p. ix.
5. Lionel Trilling, *E. M. Forster* (Norfolk, Conn.: New Directions, 1943), p. 8.
6. Conrad Knickerbocker, "Humor With a Mortal Sting," in *The World of Black Humor*, ed. Douglas M. Davis.
7. "John Barth," in *The Contemporary Writer*, ed. L. S. Dembo and Cyrena N. Pondrom, pp. 18, 19.
8. Max F. Schulz, *Black Humor Fiction of the Sixties*, p. x.
9. Bruce Janoff, "Black Humor: Beyond Satire," pp. 18, 20.
10. Leo J. Hertzel, "An Interview with Robert Coover," p. 28.
11. "John Hawkes," in *The Contemporary Writer*, ed. Dembo and Pondrom, p. 8.
12. E. D. Hirsch, *Validity in Interpretation* (New Haven, Conn.: Yale University Press, 1967), p. 74.
13. See Bruce Janoff, "Black Humor," p. 18, and Ihab Hassan, *Radical Innocence*, p. 118.
14. See Northrop Frye, *Anatomy of Criticism*, pp. 172–75; 226–28, for a discussion of these comic types.
15. Mark Twain, *The Adventures of Huckleberry Finn* (New York: Charles L. Webster & Co., 1885), pp. 135–36.
16. J. P. Donleavy, *The Ginger Man* (1955; paperback reprint, New York: Delacorte Press, 1965), p. 132.
17. Dale Underwood, *Etherege and the Seventeenth-Century Comedy of Manners* (New Haven, Conn.: Yale University Press, 1957), pp. 107–8.
18. Hassan, *Radical Innocence*, p. 117.
19. See "John Hawkes," in *The Contemporary Writer*, ed. Dembo and Pondrom, p. 8. Hawkes insists that evil is one of the "pure words" he means to "preserve."
20. Robert Coover, *The Universal Baseball Association, Inc. J. Henry Waugh, Prop.*, (New York: New American Library, 1971), p. 37.
21. Henri Bergson, "Laughter," in *Comedy*, ed. Sypher, p. 105.
22. Thomas Pynchon, *V* (1963; paperback reprint, New York: Bantam Books, 1964), p. 265.
23. Joseph Heller, *Catch-22* (1961; paperback reprint, New York: Dell Publishing Co., 1962), p. 75.
24. Vladimir Nabokov, *Lolita* (New York: G. P. Putnam's Sons, 1958), p. 150.
25. Purdy, *Cabot Wright Begins*, p. 170.
26. Heller, *Catch-22*, p. 184.
27. Molière, *The Mock-Doctor*, in *Molière's Comedies* (London: J. M. Dent & Sons, 1965), 1:415.

28. Molière, *Love's the Best Doctor*, in *Molière's Comedies*, 2:65.
29. Robert Scholes, *The Fabulators*, p. 41.
30. Richard Poirier, "The Politics of Self-Parody," pp. 339–53.
31. Frye, *Anatomy of Criticism*, p. 44: "In the figure of Prospero we have one of the few approaches to the Aristophanic technique of having the whole comic action projected by a central character."
32. Purdy, *Cabot Wright Begins*, p. 194.
33. "John Hawkes," in *The Contemporary Writer*, ed. Dembo and Pondrom, p. 3.
34. "John Barth," in *The Contemporary Writer*, ed. Dembo and Pondrom, p. 23.
35. Ibid., p. 21.
36. Jorge Luis Borges, *Labyrinths* (New York: New Directions Publishing Corp., 1964), p. 13.
37. L. J. Potts, *Comedy*, p. 78.
38. Nabokov, *Lolita*, p. 11.
39. Ibid., p. 119.
40. Ibid., p. 306.
41. John Barth, *The Floating Opera* (New York: Bantam Books, 1972), p. 101.
42. W. C. Fields, quoted in Hamlin Hill, "Black humor: its cause and cure," p. 57.
43. Sypher, "Meanings of Comedy," p. 214.
44. Walter Kerr, *Tragedy and Comedy*, p. 17.
45. "John Hawkes," in *The Contemporary Writer*, ed. Dembo and Pondrom, pp. 5–6.
46. Potts, *Comedy*, p. 47.
47. Robert W. Corrigan, *Comedy: Meaning and Form*, p. 245.
48. Kerr, *Tragedy and Comedy*, pp. 318–19.
49. Scholes, *The Fabulators*, p. 43.
50. Wylie Sypher, *The Loss of the Self in Modern Literature*, pp. 155–56.

Notes to Chapter II.

1. John Barth, *The Floating Opera*, (New York: Bantam Books, 1972), pp. 56–57. References to the 1956 edition are from Barth, *The Floating Opera* (New York: Avon Books, 1969). Subsequent references are in the text.
2. Campbell Tatham, "John Barth and the Aesthetics of Artifice," p. 65.
3. Stanley Edgar Hyman, "John Barth's First Novel," *The New Leader*, 12 April 1965, p. 21.
4. John C. Stubbs, "John Barth as a Novelist of Ideas: The Themes of Value and Identity," pp. 101–16.
5. W. L. Godshalk, "Cabell and Barth: Our Comic Athletes," in *The Comic Imagination in American Literature*, ed. Louis D. Rubin, Jr., p. 283.
6. Quoted in Judith Golwyn, "New Creative Writers," *Library Journal* 81 (June 1956):1496.

7. For a discussion of these comic archetypes see Northrop Frye, *Anatomy of Criticism*, pp. 172–75; 226–28.
8. George Meredith, "An Essay on Comedy," in *Comedy*, ed. Wylie Sypher, p. 48.
9. See Dennis M. Martin, "Desire and Disease: The Psychological Pattern of *The Floating Opera*," pp. 17–33.
10. See my Chapter I, p. 9.
11. Jorge Luis Borges, *Labyrinths* (New York: New Directions Publishing Corp., 1964), p. 208.

Notes to Chapter III.

1. "John Hawkes: An Interview," in *Studies in "Second Skin,"* ed. John Graham, p. 27.
2. Ibid.
3. Albert J. Guerard, "*Second Skin*: The Light and Dark Affirmation," in *Studies in "Second Skin,"* ed. Graham, p. 94.
4. Susan Sontag, "Review of Second Skin," in *Studies in "Second Skin,"* ed. Graham, p. 3.
5. Thomas LeClair, "The Unreliability of Innocence: John Hawkes' *Second Skin*," p. 38.
6. John Kuehl, "Story into Novel," in *Studies in "Second Skin,"* ed. Graham, p. 37.
7. Peter Brooks, "Review of *Second Skin*," in *Studies in "Second Skin,"* ed. Graham, p. 16.
8. For an important exception see Donald J. Greiner, *Comic Terror*, pp. 159–201.
9. See my Chapter I, p. 9.
10. John Hawkes, *Second Skin* (New York: New Directions, 1964), p. 3; subsequent references are in the text.
11. John Graham, "Preface" to *Studies in "Second Skin,"* p. v.
12. Walter Kerr, *Comedy and Tragedy*, p. 328.
13. "John Hawkes: An Interview," p. 27.
14. For a discussion of this comic form see Northrop Frye, *Anatomy of Criticism*, pp. 163–86.
15. "John Hawkes: An Interview," p. 26.
16. John Graham, "John Hawkes: On His Novels," in *Studies in "Second Skin,"* ed. Graham, p. 32.
17. Aldous Huxley, *Eyeless in Gaza* (1936; paperback reprint, New York: Harper & Row, 1974), pp. 341–42.
18. William Shakespeare, *The Tempest*, in *The Complete Plays and Poems of William Shakespeare*, ed. William Allan Neilson and Charles Jarvis Hill (Cambridge: Houghton Mifflin Co., 1942), act 5, sc. 1, lines 25–28.
19. Stanley Kaufmann, "Review of *Second Skin*," in *Studies in "Second Skin,"* ed. Graham, p. 6.
20. *The Tempest*, act 4, sc. 1, line 188.
21. Ibid., act 2, sc. 2, lines 316, 323.

22. Ibid., act 2, sc. 2, lines 49, 52.
23. John Hawkes and Robert Scholes, "A Conversation on *The Blood Oranges*," p. 197.
24. *The Tempest*, act 1, sc. 2, line 93.
25. Ibid., act 4, sc. 1, lines 15–22.
26. "John Hawkes: An Interview," p. 29.
27. Hawkes and Scholes, "A Conversation," p. 197.
28. "John Hawkes: An Interview," p. 27.

Notes to Chapter IV.

1. See Alfred Appel, Jr., *The Annotated Lolita*, and Carl R. Proffer, *Keys to Lolita.*
2. Lionel Trilling, "The Last Lover: Vladimir Nabokov's *Lolita*," p. 11.
3. Ibid., p. 15.
4. Ibid., p. 19.
5. Andrew Field, *Nabokov: His Life in Art*, pp. 330, 331.
6. Donald E. Morton, *Vladimir Nabokov*, p. 71.
7. G. D. Josipovici, "Lolita: Parody and the Pursuit of Beauty," p. 38.
8. Vladimir Nabokov, *Lolita* (New York: G. P. Putnam's Sons, 1958), p. 7; subsequent references are in the text.
9. Kingsley Amis, *What Became of Jane Austen?*, p. 78.
10. Ibid., p. 82.
11. F. W. Dupee, *The King of the Cats*, p. 118.
12. E. D. Hirsch, Jr., *Validity in Interpretation* (New Haven, Conn.: Yale University Press, 1967), p. 74.
13. Trilling, "The Last Lover," p. 19.
14. Howard Nemerov, "The Morality of Art," in his *Poetry and Fiction: Essays*, p. 261.
15. Daniel J. Hughes, "Reality and the Hero: Lolita and Henderson," p. 345.
16. Dupee, *King of the Cats*, p. 119.
17. Alfred Appel, Jr., "*Lolita*: The Springboard of Parody," in *Nabokov: The Man and his Work*, ed. L. S. Dembo, p. 115.
18. Ibid., p. 120.
19. Dupee, *King of the Cats*, p. 125.
20. Page Stegner, *Escape Into Aesthetics: The Art of Vladimir Nabokov*, p. 114.
21. Richard Pearce, *Stages of the Clown*, p. 101.
22. Robert W. Uphaus, "Nabokov's Kunstlerroman: Portrait of the Artist as a Dying Man," p. 104.
23. Dupee, *King of the Cats*, p. 128.
24. Review of *Lolita* in *Time*, 1 September 1958, p. 64.
25. Field, *Nabokov*, p. 347.
26. Vladimir Nabokov, *Strong Opinions*, p. 94.
27. James Joyce, *A Portrait of the Artist as a Young Man* (1916; paperback reprint, New York: The Viking Press, 1964), p. 70.
28. Alfred Appel, Jr., "An Interview with Vladimir Nabokov," in *Nabokov*, ed. Dembo, p. 42.

29. Dorothy Van Ghent, *The English Novel: Form and Function* (1953; paperback reprint, New York: Harper & Row, 1967), pp. 21–22, 23–24.

30. Vladimir Nabokov, *The Real Life of Sebastian Knight* (Norfolk, Conn.: New Directions, 1959), p. 91.

Notes to Chapter V.

1. Marcia L. Falk, "Letter to the Editor of *The New York Times*," in *One Flew Over the Cuckoo's Nest*, ed. John C. Pratt, p. 452.

2. See Janet Sutherland, "A Defense of Ken Kesey's *One Flew Over the Cuckoo's Nest*," pp. 128–36.

3. Raymond M. Olderman, *Beyond the Waste Land: The American Novel in the Nineteen-Sixties*, p. 50.

4. Bruce E. Wallis, "Christ in the Cuckoo's Nest: Or, The Gospel According to Ken Kesey," pp. 52–58.

5. Ken Kesey, *One Flew Over the Cuckoo's Nest*, (New York: Viking Press, 1962), p. 3; subsequent references are in the text.

6. See Northrop Frye, *Anatomy of Criticism*, pp. 172–75, 226–28.

7. F. M. Cornford, *The Origin of Attic Comedy*, ed. Theodore Gaster (Garden City, N.Y.: Doubleday & Co., 1961), p. 9.

8. Wylie Sypher, ed., *Comedy*, p. 221.

9. Ibid., p. 202.

10. Morton Gurewitch, *Comedy: The Irrational Vision*, p. 56.

11. Ibid.

12. Sypher, ed., *Comedy*, p. 220.

13. Ibid.

14. Wallis, "Christ in the Cuckoo's Nest," p. 52.

15. See my Chapter I, p. 9.

16. Robert Boyers, "Porno Politics," in *One Flew Over the Cuckoo's Nest*, ed. Pratt, p. 439.

17. Ibid., p. 441.

18. Ruth H. Brady, "Kesey's *One Flew Over the Cuckoo's Nest*," *Explicator* 31, no. 6 (February 1973), item 41.

19. Ken Kesey, "Letter to Ken Babbs," in *One Flew Over the Cuckoo's Nest*, ed. Pratt, p. 339.

20. Joseph Heller, *Catch-22* (1961; paperback reprint, New York: Dell Publishing Co., 1962), p. 45.

21. Leslie Fiedler, *The Return of the Vanishing American*, pp. 182–83.

22. Sypher, *Comedy*, p. 200.

23. Ken Kesey, "An Impolite Interview with Ken Kesey," in *One Flew Over the Cuckoo's Nest*, ed. Pratt, p. 353.

Notes to Chapter VI.

1. Leo J. Hertzel, "An Interview with Robert Coover," p. 28.

2. Red Smith, Review of *The Universal Baseball Association* in *Best Sellers*, 1 August 1968, p. 170.

3. Neil Schmitz, "Robert Coover and the Hazards of Metafiction," p. 213.
4. Jackson I. Cope, "Robert Coover's Fictions," p. 105.
5. Max F. Schulz, *Black Humor Fiction of the Sixties*, p. 138.
6. Robert Coover, *The Universal Baseball Association, Inc. J. Henry Waugh, Prop.* (New York: New American Library, 1971), p. 44; subsequent references are in the text.
7. David Quentin Voigt, *American Baseball* (Norman: University of Oklahoma Press, 1966), p. 15.
8. For further historical background see Voigt, *American Baseball*, pp. 6–7, 8, 25–28, 30–34, and Lee Allen, *100 Years of Baseball* (New York: Bartholomew House, 1950), pp. 11–34.
9. Quoted in Voigt, *American Baseball*, p. 6.
10. Ibid., p. 5.
11. Hy Turkin and S. C. Thompson, *The Official Encyclopedia of Baseball* (New York: A. S. Barnes & Co., 1963), pp. 1–2.
12. Both Cope, "Robert Coover's Fictions," and Schulz, *Black Humor Fiction*, assume that Jock Casey is Christ.
13. Robert Coover, *Pricksongs & Descants* (New York: E. P. Dutton & Co., 1969), p. 78.

Notes to Chapter VII.

1. James Purdy, *Cabot Wright Begins* (New York: Farrar, Straus & Giroux, 1964), p. 200.
2. Joseph Heller, "An Interview in New York with Joseph Heller," *Studies in the Novel* 4, no. 1 (Spring 1972):73.
3. Philip Roth, *Portnoy's Complaint* (New York: Random House, 1969), p. 265.
4. Elliott Baker, *A Fine Madness* (New York: G. P. Putnam's Sons, 1964), p. 220.
5. "John Hawkes," in *The Contemporary Writer*, ed. L. S. Dembo and Cyrena N. Pondrom, p. 3.
6. Kurt Vonnegut, Jr., *God Bless You, Mr. Rosewater or Pearls Before Swine* (New York: Holt, Rinehart & Winston, 1965), p. 47.
7. Vladimir Nabokov, *Pale Fire* (New York: G. P. Putnam's Sons, 1962), p. 212.
8. Conrad Knickerbocker, "Humor With a Mortal Sting," in *The World of Black Humor*, ed. Douglas M. Davis, p. 299.
9. Baker, *A Fine Madness*, pp. 318, 274.
10. Rita Mae Brown, *Rubyfruit Jungle* (1973; paperback reprint, New York: Bantam Books, 1977), p. 246.
11. L. J. Potts, *Comedy*, p. 11.
12. Robert Scholes, *The Fabulators*, p. 45.
13. Bruce Jay Friedman, *Stern* (New York; Simon & Schuster, 1962), p. 157.
14. Roth, *Portnoy's Complaint*, p. 134.
15. Purdy, *Cabot Wright Begins*, p. 213.

Selected Bibliography

The Novels

A Note on the Editions Cited

For the five novels discussed in detail, I have used editions currently in print. *Lolita* and *One Flew Over the Cuckoo's Nest* are available in the first American hardback editions. *The Floating Opera, Second Skin,* and *The Universal Baseball Association, Inc. J. Henry Waugh, Prop.* are available only in paperback editions.

Barth, John. *The Floating Opera.* New York: Appleton-Century-Crofts, 1956. Reprint, New York: Avon Books, 1969. Rev. ed. by author. New York: Doubleday & Co., 1967. Reprint, New York: Bantam Books, 1972.

Coover, Robert. *The Universal Baseball Association, Inc. J. Henry Waugh, Prop.* New York; Random House, 1968. Reprint, New York: New American Library, 1971.

Hawkes, John. *Second Skin.* New York: New Directions, 1964.

Kesey, Ken. *One Flew Over the Cuckoo's Nest.* New York: Viking Press, 1962.

Nabokov, Vladimir. *Lolita.* Paris: The Olympia Press, 1955. 1st American ed. New York: G. P. Putnam's Sons, 1958.

General Works

Allen, Mary. *The Necessary Blankness: Women in Major American Fiction of the Sixties.* Urbana: University of Illinois Press, 1976.

"American Humor: Hardly a Laughing Matter." Time, 4 March 1966, pp. 46–47.

Baumbach, Jonathan. *The Landscape of Nightmare: Studies in the Contemporary American Novel.* New York: New York University Press, 1965.

Blair, Walter, and Hill, Hamlin. *America's Humor from Poor Richard to Doonesbury.* New York: Oxford University Press, 1978.

Breton, André. *Anthologie de l'humour noir.* 1939. Reprint, Paris: Jean-Jacques Pauvert, 1966.

Bridgman, Richard. "Satire's Changing Target." *College Composition and Communication* 16 (May 1965):85–89.

Chase, Richard. *The American Novel and Its Tradition.* New York: Doubleday, Anchor Books, 1957.

Corrigan, Robert W. *Comedy: Meaning and Form.* San Francisco: Chandler Publishing Co., 1965.

Davis, Douglas M., ed. *The World of Black Humor: An Introductory Anthology of Selections and Criticisms.* New York: E. P. Dutton & Co., 1969.

Davis, Robert M. "The Shrinking Garden and New Exits: The Comic Satiric Novel in the Twentieth Century." *Kansas Quarterly* 1 (Summer 1969):5–16.

Dembo, L. S., and Pondrom, Cyrena N. *The Contemporary Writer: Interviews with Sixteen Novelists and Poets.* Madison: University of Wisconsin Press, 1972.

Feldman, Burton. "The Anatomy of Black Humor." *Dissent* 15 (March–April, 1968):158–60.

Fiedler, Leslie. "The Black Humorists." *Time*, 12 February 1965, p. 94.

Frye, Northrop. *Anatomy of Criticism.* 1957. Paperback reprint, Princeton, N.J.: Princeton University Press, 1971.

Galloway, David D. *The Absurd Hero in American Fiction.* Austin: University of Texas Press, 1970.

Gindin, James. "Well Beyond Laughter: Directions from Fifties Comic Fiction." *Studies in the Novel* 3 (Winter 1971):357–64.

Gurewitch, Morton. *Comedy: The Irrational Vision.* Ithaca, N.Y.: Cornell University Press, 1975.

Hassan, Ihab. "Laughter in the Dark." *American Scholar* 33 (Autumn 1964):636–40.

———. *Radical Innocence.* Princeton, N.J.: Princeton University Press, 1961.

Hill, Hamlin. "Black Humor and the Mass Audience." In *American Humor: Essays Presented to John C. Gerber*, edited by O. M. Brock, Jr., Scottsdale, Ariz.: Arete Publications, 1977.

———. "Black humor: its cause and cure." *The Colorado Quarterly* 17 (Summer 1968):57–64.

———. "Modern American Humor." *College English* 25 (December 1963):170–76.

Janoff, Bruce. "Black Humor: Beyond Satire." *Ohio Review* 14 (Fall 1972):5–20.

Kerr, Walter. *Tragedy and Comedy.* New York: Simon & Schuster, 1967.

Klein, Marcus. *The American Novel Since World War Two.* Greenwich, Conn.: Fawcett Publishing Co., 1969.

Kostelanetz, Richard, ed. *On Contemporary Literature.* New York: Avon Books, 1969.

LeClair, Thomas. "Final Words: Death and Comedy in the Fiction of Donleavy, Hawkes, Barth, and Vonnegut." Ph.D. dissertation, Duke University, 1973.

Maddocks, Melvin. "We Are Not Amused—And Why." *Time*, 20 July 1970, pp. 30–31.

Martin, Robert Bernard. "Notes Toward a Comic Fiction." In *The*

Theory of the Novel, edited by John Halperin. New York: Oxford University Press, 1974.

Meeker, Joseph W. "The Comedy of Survival." *The North American Review* 9 (Summer 1972):11–17.

Olderman, Raymond M. *Beyond the Wasteland: The American Novel in the Nineteen-Sixties*. New Haven, Conn.: Yale University Press, 1972.

Pearce, Richard. *Stages of the Clown: Perspectives on Modern Fiction from Dostoevsky to Beckett*. Carbondale and Edwardsville: Southern Illinois University Press, 1970.

Pinsker, Sanford. "The Greying of Black Humor." *Studies in the Twentieth Century* 9 (Spring 1972):15–33.

Poirier, Richard. "The Politics of Self-Parody." *Partisan Review* 35 (Summer 1968):339–53.

———. *A World Elsewhere*. New York: Oxford University Press, 1966.

Potts, L. J. *Comedy*. London: Hutchinson's University Library, 1948.

Rubin, Louis D., Jr., ed. *The Comic Imagination in American Literature*. New Brunswick, N.J.: Rutgers University Press, 1973.

Scholes, Robert. *The Fabulators*. New York: Oxford University Press, 1967.

Schulz, Max F. *Black Humor Fiction of the Sixties*. Athens: Ohio University Press, 1973.

———. "Toward a Definition of Black Humor." *Southern Review* 9 (Winter 1973):117–34.

Shulman, Max. "American Humor: Its Cause and Cure." *Yale Review* 51 (Autumn 1961):119–24.

Shulman, Robert. "Myth, Mr. Eliot, and the Comic Novel." *Modern Fiction Studies* 12 (Winter 1966–1967):395–403.

Stuart, Dabney. "Laughter in the Dark: Parody." *TriQuarterly* 17 (Winter 1970):72–95.

Sypher, Wylie, ed. *Comedy: "An Essay on Comedy" by George Meredith, "Laughter" by Henri Bergson*. Introduction and Appendix ("The Meanings of Comedy") by Wylie Sypher. Garden City, N.Y.: Doubleday & Co., 1956.

———. *The Loss of the Self in Modern Literature*. New York: Random House, 1962.

Tanner, Tony. *City of Words: American Fiction, 1950–1970*. New York: Harper & Row, 1971.

Thurber, James. "The Future, If Any, of Comedy." *Harper's*, December 1961, pp. 40–45.

Tilton, John W. *Cosmic Satire in the Contemporary American Novel*. Lewisburg, Pa.: Bucknell University Press, 1977.

Trachtenberg, Stanley. "Counterhumor: Comedy in Contemporary American Fiction." *Georgia Review* 27 (Spring 1973):33–48.

Welsford, Enid. *The Fool.* Garden City, N.Y.: Doubleday, Anchor Books, 1961.

The Floating Opera

Gerhard, Joseph. *John Barth.* Minneapolis: University of Minnesota Press, 1970.

Gross, Beverly, "The Anti-Novels of John Barth." *Chicago Review* 20 (November 1968):95–109.

Harris, Charles B. "Todd Andrews: Ontological Insecurity, and *The Floating Opera.*" *Critique* 18, no. 2 (1976):34–50.

Hauck, Richard B. *A Cheerful Nihilism.* Bloomington: Indiana University Press, 1971.

Hicks, Granville. "John Barth." In his *Literary Horizons*, pp. 257–72. New York: New York University Press, 1970.

Kennard, Jean E. "John Barth: Imitations of Imitations." *Mosaic* 3 (Winter 1970):116–31.

Korkowski, Eugene. "The Excremental Vision of Barth's Todd Andrews." *Critique* 18, no. 2 (1976):51–58.

LeClair, Thomas. "John Barth's *The Floating Opera*: Death and the Craft of Fiction." *Texas Studies in Literature and Language* 14 (Winter 1973):711–30.

Martin, Dennis M. "Desire and Disease: The Psychological Pattern of *The Floating Opera.*" *Critique* 18, no. 2 (1976):17–33.

Morrell, David. *John Barth: An Introduction.* University Park: Pennsylvania State University Press, 1976.

Noland, Richard W. "John Barth and the Novel of Comic Nihilism." *Contemporary Literature* 7 (Autumn 1966):239–57.

Rovit, Earl. "The Novel as Parody: John Barth." *Critique* 6 (Fall 1963):77–85.

Ryan, Marjorie. "Four Contemporary Satires." *Satire Newsletter* 6 (Spring 1969):40–46.

Schickel, Richard. "The Floating Opera." *Critique* 6 (Fall 1963):53–67.

Stubbs, John C. "John Barth as a Novelist of Ideas: The Themes of Value and Identity." *Critique* 8, no. 2 (Winter 1965–1966):101–16.

Tanner, Stephen L. "John Barth's Hamlet." *Southwest Review* 56 (Autumn 1971):347–54.

Tatham, Campbell. "John Barth and the Aesthetics of Artifice." *Contemporary Literature* 12 (Winter 1971):60–73.

Trachtenberg, Alan. "Barth and Hawkes: Two Fabulists." *Critique* 6 (Fall 1963):4–18.

Second Skin

Bassoff, Bruce. "Mythic Truth and Deception in *Second Skin.*" *Etudes Anglaise* 30 (July–September 1977):337–42.

Busch, Fred. *Hawkes: A Guide to His Fictions.* Syracuse, N.Y.: Syracuse University Press, 1973.
Emmett, Paul, and Vine, Richard. "A Conversation with John Hawkes." *Chicago Review* 28 (Fall 1976):163–71.
Frohock, W. M. "John Hawkes' Vision of Violence." *Southwest Review* 50 (Winter 1965):69–79.
Graham, John, ed. *Studies in "Second Skin."* Columbus, Ohio: Charles E. Merrill Publishing Co., 1971.
Greiner, Donald J. *Comic Terror: The Novels of John Hawkes.* Memphis, Tenn.: Memphis State University Press, 1973.
Guerard, Albert J. "The Prose Style of John Hawkes." *Critique* 6 (Fall 1963):19–29.
Hawkes, John. "Flannery O'Connor's Devil." *Sewanee Review* 70 (Summer 1962):395–407.
Hawkes, John, and Scholes, Robert. "A Conversation on *The Blood Oranges.*" *Novel* 5 (Spring 1972):197–207.
Kuehl, John. *John Hawkes and the Craft of Conflict.* New Brunswick, N.J.: Rutgers University Press, 1975.
Laing, Jeffrey M. "The Upturned Smile: Comic Strategies in the Fiction of John Hawkes." *Gypsy Scholar* 4 (1977):123–29.
Lavers, Norman. "The Structure of *Second Skin.*" *Novel* 5 (Spring 1972):208–14.
LeClair, Thomas. "The Unreliability of Innocence: John Hawkes' *Second Skin.*" *Journal of Narrative Technique* 3 (January 1973):32–39.
Matthews, Charles. "The Destructive Vision of John Hawkes." *Critique* 6 (Fall 1963):38–52.
Rovit, Earl. "The Fiction of John Hawkes: An Introductory View." *Modern Fiction Studies* 11 (Summer 1964):150–62.
Stubbs, John C. "John Hawkes and the Dream-Work of *The Lime Twig* and *Second Skin.*" *Literature and Psychology* 21, no. 3 (1971):149–60.

Lolita

Amis, Kingsley. *What Became of Jane Austen?* New York: Harcourt Brace Jovanovich, 1970.
Appel, Alfred, Jr. *The Annotated Lolita.* New York: McGraw-Hill Book Co., 1970.
———. *Nabokov.* Evanston, Ill.: Northwestern University Press 1970.
Bader, Julia. *Crystal Land.* Berkeley: University of California Press, 1972.
Dembo, L. S., ed. *Nabokov: The Man and His Work.* Madison: University of Wisconsin Press, 1967.
Dupee, F. W. *The King of the Cats.* New York: Farrar, Straus & Giroux, 1965.

Fiedler, Leslie. *Love and Death in the American Novel.* New York: Criterion Books, 1960.
Field, Andrew. *Nabokov: His Life in Art.* Boston: Little, Brown & Co., 1967.
Fowler, Douglas. *Reading Nabokov.* Ithaca, N.Y.: Cornell University Press, 1974.
Hughes, Daniel J. "Reality and the Hero: Lolita and Henderson." *Modern Fiction Studies* 6, no. 4 (Winter 1960–1961):345–64.
Josipovici, G. D. "Lolita: Parody and the Pursuit of Beauty." *Critical Quarterly* 6 (Spring 1964):35–48.
McDonald, James L. "John Ray, Jr., Critic and Artist: The Foreword to *Lolita.*" *Studies in the Novel* 5 (Fall 1973):352–57.
Mitchell, Charles. "Mythic Seriousness in *Lolita.*" *Texas Studies in Literature and Language* 5 (Autumn 1963):329–43.
Morton, Donald E. *Vladimir Nabokov.* New York: Frederick Ungar Publishing Co., 1974.
Nabokov, Vladimir. *Strong Opinions.* New York: McGraw-Hill Book Co., 1973.
Nemerov, Howard. "The Morality of Art." In his *Poetry and Fiction: Essays,* pp. 260–66. New Brunswick, N.J.: Rutgers University Press, 1963.
Proffer, Carl R. *Keys to Lolita.* Bloomington: Indiana University Press, 1968.
Rubman, Lewis H. "Creatures and Creators in *Lolita* and 'Death and the Compass.'" *Modern Fiction Studies* 19 (Autumn 1973):433–52.
Stegner, Page. *Escape into Aesthetics: The Art of Vladimir Nabokov.* New York: The Dial Press, 1966.
Trilling, Lionel. "The Last Lover: Vladimir Nabokov's *Lolita.*" *Encounter* 11, no. 4 (October 1958):9–19.
Uphaus, Robert W. "Nabokov's Kunstlerroman: Portrait of the Artist as a Dying Man." *Twentieth Century Literature* 13 (July 1967):104–10.

One Flew Over the Cuckoo's Nest

Beidler, Peter G., and Hunt, John W., eds. "Perspectives on a Cuckoo's Nest: A Symposium on Ken Kesey." *Lex et Scientia* 13, nos. 1 and 2 (1977).
Blessing, Richard. "The Moving Target: Ken Kesey's Evolving Hero." *Journal of Popular Culture* 4 (Fall 1970):615–27.
Fiedler, Leslie A. *The Return of the Vanishing American.* New York: Stein & Day, 1968.
Hauck, Richard B. "The Comic Christ and the Modern Reader." *College English* 31 (February 1970):498–506.
Hoge, James O. "Psychedelic Stimulation and the Creative Imagina-

tion: The Case of Ken Kesey." *Southern Humanities Review* 6 (Fall 1972):381–91.

Kunz, Don R. "Mechanistic and Totemistic Symbolization in Kesey's *One Flew Over the Cuckoo's Nest.*" *Studies in American Fiction* 13 (Spring 1975):65–82.

Martin, Terrence. "*One Flew Over the Cuckoo's Nest* and the High Cost of Living." *Modern Fiction Studies* 19 (Spring 1973):43–55.

Mills, Nicolaus. "Ken Kesey and the Politics of Laughter." *Centennial Review* 16 (Winter 1972):82–90.

Pearson, Carol. "The Cowboy Saint and the Indian Poet: The Comic Hero in Ken Kesey's *One Flew Over the Cuckoo's Nest.*" *Studies in American Humor* 1 (October 1974):91–98.

Pratt, John C., ed. *One Flew Over the Cuckoo's Nest: Text and Criticism.* New York: Viking Press, 1973.

Sherman, W. D. "The Novels of Ken Kesey." *Journal of American Studies* 5, no. 2 (1971):185–96.

Sherwood, Terry G. "*One Flew Over the Cuckoo's Nest* and the Comic Strip." *Critique* 13, no. 1 (1970):96–109.

Sutherland, Janet. "A Defense of Ken Kesey's *One Flew Over the Cuckoo's Nest.*" *English Journal* 61 (January 1972):128–36.

Tanner, Stephen L. "Salvation Through Laughter: Ken Kesey and the Cuckoo's Nest." *Southwest Review* 58 (Spring 1973):125–37.

Waldmeir, Joseph J. "Two Novelists of the Absurd: Heller and Kesey." *Contemporary Literature* 5 (Autumn 1964):192–204.

Wallis, Bruce E. "Christ in the Cuckoo's Nest: Or, The Gospel According to Ken Kesey." *Cithara* 12 (November 1972):52–58.

The Universal Baseball Association

Angelius, Judith Wood. "The Man Behind the Catcher's Mask: A Closer Look at Robert Coover's *Universal Baseball Association.*" *University of Denver Quarterly* 12, no. 1 (1977):165–74.

Cope, Jackson I. "Robert Coover's Fictions." *The Iowa Review* 2 (Summer 1971):94–110.

Gass, William H. *Fiction and the Figures of Life*, pp. 104–9. New York: Alfred A. Knopf, 1970.

Gilman, Richard. "News from the Novel." *New Republic*, 17 August 1968, p. 35.

Hansen, Arlen J. "The Dice of God: Einstein, Heisenberg, and Robert Coover." *Novel* 10 (Fall 1976):49–58.

Hertzel, Leo J. "An Interview With Robert Coover." *Critique* 11, no. 3 (1969):25–29.

———. "What's Wrong With The Christians." *Critique* 11, no. 3 (1969):11–22.

Schmitz, Neil. "Robert Coover and the Hazards of Metafiction." *Novel* 7 (Spring 1974):210–19.

Scholes, Robert. "Metafiction." *The Iowa Review* 1 (Fall 1970):100–115.
Sheed, Wilfrid. "A New Ballgame." *New York Times Book Review*, 7 July 1968, p. 5.
Shelton, Frank W. "Humor and Balance in Coover's *The Universal Baseball Association, Inc.*" *Critique* 17 (December 1975):78–90.

Index

R

S

T

U

V

W